40 Fun-tabulous Puzzles

for Multiplication, Division, Decimals, Fractions & More!

by Bob Olenych

SCHOLASTIC
PROFESSIONAL BOOKS

New York • Toronto • London • Auckland • Sydney
Mexico City • New Delhi • Hong Kong

Dedication:

To all the students I've taught over the years

Cover design by Jim Sarfati
Interior design by Melinda Belter
Cover and interior illustrations by Steve Cox

ISBN 0-439-19941-7

Printed in the U.S.A.

Table of Contents

Introduction

MATH CAN BE FUN . . . FUN-TABULOUS!

We teachers know that "practice makes perfect"—especially for building computation skills. The puzzles in this book have provided excellent computation practice for my entire class and have motivated my most reluctant students. Many years of experience developing and using puzzles in the classroom have convinced me that when students are engaged by activities such as the puzzles in this book, they will learn effectively and tackle new challenges. While my students are "having fun" solving riddles and working through mazes, they also are building essential skills: addition, subtraction, multiplication and division—the building blocks of mathematics.

WHAT YOU'LL FIND IN THIS BOOK

This book of 40 puzzles is organized by skill areas and includes: number concepts, addition, subtraction, multiplication, division, order of operations, fractions and decimals, graphing, and time. Each section targets particular subskills, which are listed in the table of contents as well as on the practice pages.

CONNECTIONS TO THE MATH STANDARDS

Most of the puzzles in this book target *NCTM 2000* objectives listed under the Number and Operations standard. These objectives include understanding ways to represent numbers, determining meanings of operations and how they relate to one another, and computing with fluency and accuracy. This book is packed with exercises that require students to use the basic operations (addition, subtraction, multiplication, and division) in a variety of patterns—with whole numbers, decimals, and fractions.

"Riddle Time" and other puzzles feature variables, symbols, and graphs that require students to use strategies outlined in the objectives listed under the Algebra standard. Such strategies include understanding patterns, relations, and functions, and analyzing mathematical equations that use variables.

HOW TO USE THIS BOOK

I've been able to use these puzzles to meet a number of instructional goals: I usually assign one of these puzzles as a follow-up to a lesson. I also use these puzzles as review sheets and quizzes to monitor my students' progress in a specific skill area. And because these puzzles are self-correcting, they make ideal independent and homework assignments; a correct assignment will provide a solution to a riddle or a perfect match for numbers in a puzzle. If a student's answer does not correspond with one of the answers provided or it creates a glitch in the riddle, students realize that they've made an error and will double-check their work to arrive at the right solution.

My students eagerly await math period and frequently ask for these puzzles. I'm confident that your students will enjoy and benefit from this collection, too.

Bob Olenych

Name______________________________ Date ________ **NUMBER CONCEPTS**

Reveal a Historical Fact

Rewriting words as numbers; place value

Express each number below in its numerical form. Then find your answers in the grid below and cross them out. Answers run horizontally, left to right. Starting from the top left, locate each of the remaining letters and print them in order in the boxes at the bottom: The 41 boxes that are left over will reveal a secret message!

1. Two thousand six hundred eleven ____________________

2. Thirty-four thousand eighty-nine ____________________
3. Six hundred twenty-six thousand eight hundred fifty-four ____________________

4. Eight thousand eight ____________________
5. Six million five hundred thirty-four thousand two hundred eleven ____________________
6. Forty-eight million nine hundred seven thousand eight hundred sixteen ____________________
7. Five hundred eight thousand seven hundred ninety-eight ____________________
8. Eighty million one hundred sixteen thousand two hundred eleven ____________________
9. Seven thousand seven hundred seven ____________________
10. Twenty-nine thousand six hundred forty-eight ____________________

T 6	H 4	E 3	G 4	S 5	S 0	E 8	F 7	P 9	I 8	R 2	E 0	E 0	K 7
A 1	G 2	R 9	B 6	A 4	R 8	N 4	D 9	O 8	O 0	D 0	B 8	R 6	O 8
M 8	A 7	N 3	N 4	I 0	N 8	D 9	N 3	G 9	O 6	B 7	G 7	R 0	A 7
D 6	O 9	F 5	B 6	Y 5	T 3	E 4	R 2	I 1	N 1	S 7	U 1	N 0	A 9
N 4	D 0	Y 0	O 8	G 8	R 0	O 1	A 1	D 6	I 2	G 1	O 1	U 7	T 8
H 3	I 2	G 6	H 1	B 1	W 2	A 2	Y 6	R 2	I 6	B 8	S 5	O 4	S 3
A 2	P 1	O 4	T 4	R 8	I 9	M 0	S 7	H 8	E 1	R 6	L 2	L 4	O 4

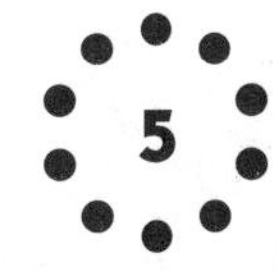

Name________________________ Date ________

NUMBER CONCEPTS

Cross-Number Puzzle

Rewriting words as numbers; place value

Change each number below to its numerical form and write your answer in the appropriate across or down position.

ACROSS

1. Four thousand seven hundred three
3. Two thousand four hundred thirty-five
4. Five thousand nine
5. One hundred sixty-four thousand five hundred ninety-three
6. Six hundred four thousand five hundred ninety
7. Eighty-five thousand three hundred ninety-six
11. Five hundred forty-six thousand three hundred seventy-one
12. Three hundred forty-eight thousand seven

DOWN

1. Four hundred ninety-three thousand six hundred sixty-six
2. Fifty thousand nine hundred thirty
4. Fifty-six thousand nine hundred thirty-four
6. Six thousand four hundred fifty-one
8. Nine thousand four hundred forty-three
9. Twenty-five thousand seven hundred ninety-three
10. Eighty-one thousand two hundred forty-seven

1 2 3 4 5 6 7 8 9 10 11 12

Name____________________ Date ________

ADDITION

Facts review

58 Errors

The addition grid below contains 58 errors. Check all of the answers. When you find a mistake, correct it and shade in that box. When you've finished shading the boxes with errors, the shaded grid will spell out the answer to the following riddle:

What always goes to bed with shoes on?

+	39	23	17	42	68	94	75	56	83	49	32	95	57	71	63
5	44	28	22	47	73	99	85	71	89	54	37	100	63	74	69
8	47	31	25	50	76	102	82	64	92	57	40	103	66	79	71
4	43	27	21	45	62	99	78	59	88	54	37	98	62	76	67
7	46	30	24	48	76	100	83	62	90	57	39	102	65	78	70
9	58	32	28	52	77	104	85	65	93	68	42	105	67	82	73
2	40	25	18	43	69	95	77	58	85	51	34	98	59	73	65
6	46	28	25	49	75	98	81	62	89	56	39	100	63	77	69
1	39	24	17	43	69	95	76	57	84	50	33	96	58	72	64
3	52	26	21	45	71	97	78	59	86	52	35	98	60	74	66

_____ _____ _____ _____ _____

Name________________________________ Date __________

ADDITION

Break the Code

3 digits/
4 addends

Solve the addition problems below. Write the answers in the across and down spaces in the cross-number puzzle. The numbers you write in the shaded boxes show where the letters should go in the code at the bottom to answer the following question:

What word has two vowels, two consonants, and two vowels—all in a row?

▶ ACROSS

2.	4.	5.	6.	8.
790	833	300	394	7,972
431	580	909	349	6,581
865	735	635	767	2,451
+ 307	+ 123	+ 471	+ 676	+ 7,632

▼ DOWN

1.	2.	3.	6.	7.
385	535	888	803	866
535	224	807	572	451
712	609	830	483	675
+ 649	+ 758	+ 826	+ 767	+ 628

	1 O		2		E	3
4		E	B			
			5	O		K
6		P				
E				7		
8	K					
				R		

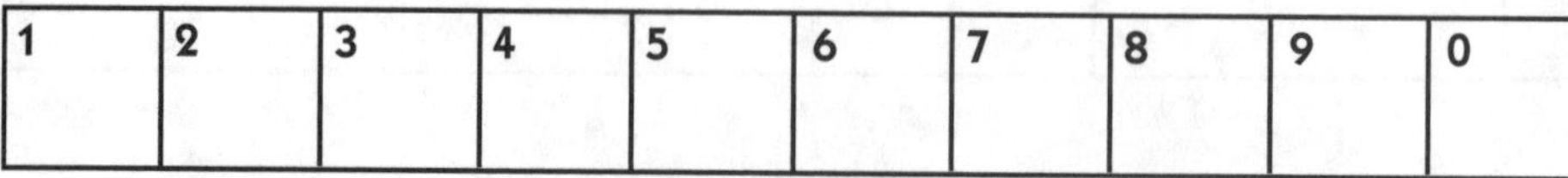

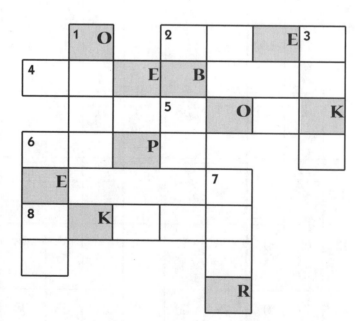

1	2	3	4	5	6	7	8	9	0

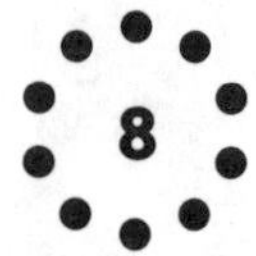

Name____________________________________ Date __________

ADDITION

4 digits/ 4 addends

"Sum" Number Search

Add each problem carefully. Locate and circle the answer—the sum—in the number search below. The answers are written horizontally and vertically.

1. 5,569 4,376 2,007 + 5,432	**2.** 8,040 4,648 3,948 + 3,205	**3.** 5,834 2,468 9,354 + 2,099	**4.** 3,603 3,063 9,066 + 9,909
5. 7,909 6,430 2,058 + 4,567	**6.** 7,777 6,666 5,005 + 6,090	**7.** 5,834 2,468 3,690 + 2,200	**8.** 5,841 2,796 7,976 + 9,797
9. 3,890 5,009 6,246 + 3,963	**10.** 5,893 2,398 5,389 + 8,477	**11.** 3,489 5,003 6,070 + 5,847	**12.** 3,347 9,969 7,800 + 7,008

2	0	9	6	4	2	6	4	1	0
5	6	9	3	1	7	3	8	4	9
6	2	2	1	5	7	3	7	1	6
4	5	8	0	2	0	4	0	9	4
1	9	8	4	1	2	8	1	2	4
6	0	1	9	7	5	5	5	7	1
2	5	5	3	8	1	9	1	0	8

Name______________________ Date ________

SUBTRACTION

4 digits

What's The Difference? Number Search

Subtract each problem carefully. Locate and circle the answer—the difference—in the number search below. The answers are written horizontally and vertically.

1. 7,906 − 4,537	2. 8,800 − 4,675	3. 14,768 − 9,794	4. 3,908 − 349	5. 6,902 − 4,768
6. 5,903 − 3,344	7. 7,990 − 6,999	8. 14,108 − 6,394	9. 7,000 − 395	10. 5,934 − 4,376
11. 7,543 − 5,097	12. 9,004 − 8,432	13. 4,567 − 3,997	14. 18,942 − 9,932	15. 5,826 − 3,455

7	6	0	6	4	3	5	7	2	4	7
7	3	3	6	9	5	7	1	5	5	8
1	6	6	0	7	9	0	5	5	3	2
4	1	2	5	4	7	8	2	9	9	1
6	9	9	0	1	0	2	4	4	6	3
3	5	5	9	6	2	3	7	1	5	4

Name________________________________ Date __________ SUBTRACTION

5 digits

Last Number–First Number #1

Solve the following subtraction problems. Write your answers in the winding puzzle below. **Note: The last digit of each answer becomes the first digit of the next answer.** Be sure to follow the arrows as you fill in the boxes, because you will have to write the following answers backward: numbers 5, 6, 7, 8, 11, and 12. After you've finished the puzzle, look at the numbers you've written in the shaded boxes. Each number shows where the letter in that box should go in the code at the bottom to answer the following question:

What geometric figure never makes a mistake?

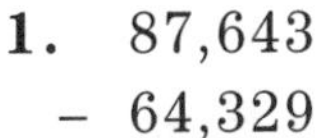

1.	2.	3.	4.	5.	6.
87,643	96,840	59,751	85,934	97,091	97,381
– 64,329	– 53,477	– 23,324	– 13,029	– 46,043	– 10,049

7.	8.	9.	10.	11.	12.
77,790	65,472	86,790	57,475	94,476	87,473
– 56,379	– 50,268	– 40,418	– 30,149	– 34,259	– 12,205

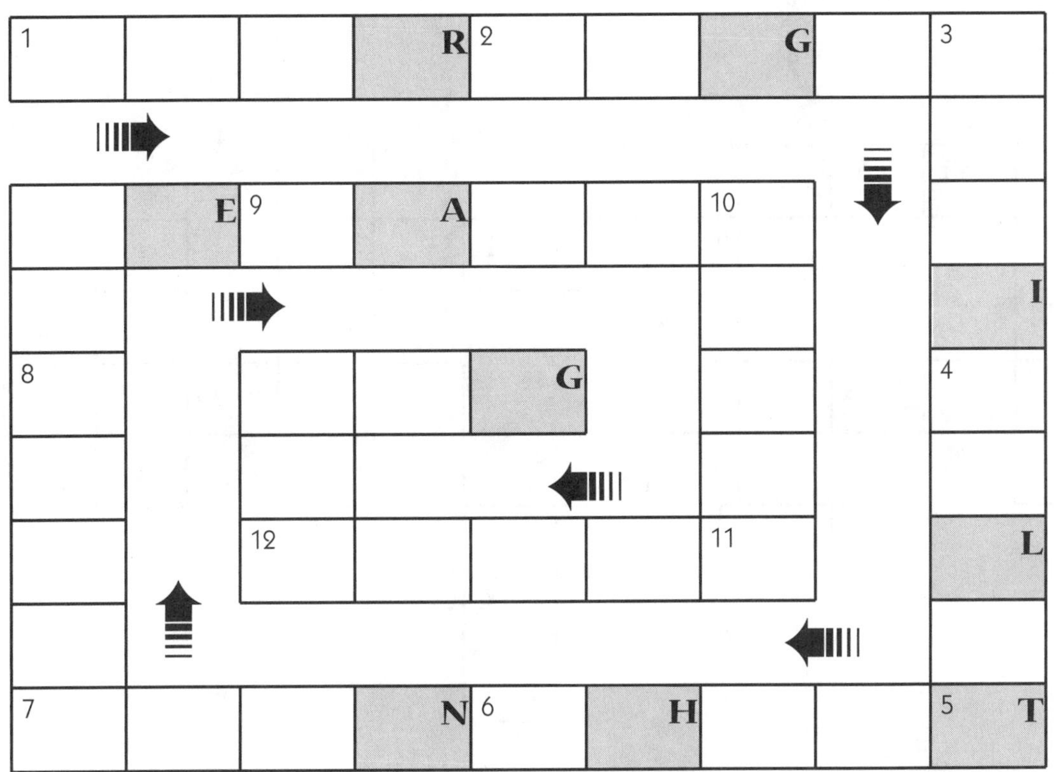

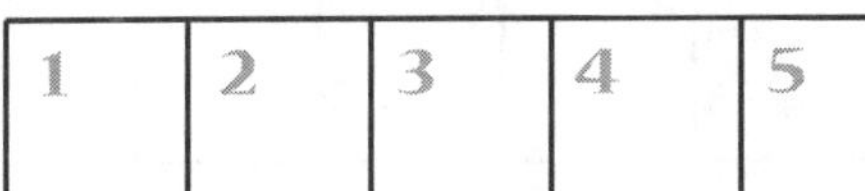

Name______________________________ Date __________

Solve the Mystery

Solve the ten subtraction problems below. Write the answers in the across and down spaces in the cross-number puzzle. The number in the shaded box shows where the letter should go in the code at the bottom to solve the following riddle:

What illness is difficult to discuss until it's completely cured?

ACROSS

1.	5.	6.	7.	9.
64,208	25,347	38,020	90,844	24,782
− 51,099	− 8,990	− 17,528	− 50,227	− 19,577

DOWN

2.	3.	4.	5.	8.
59,344	88,677	75,757	96,471	39,007
− 27,422	− 61,368	− 31,339	− 84,249	− 35,455

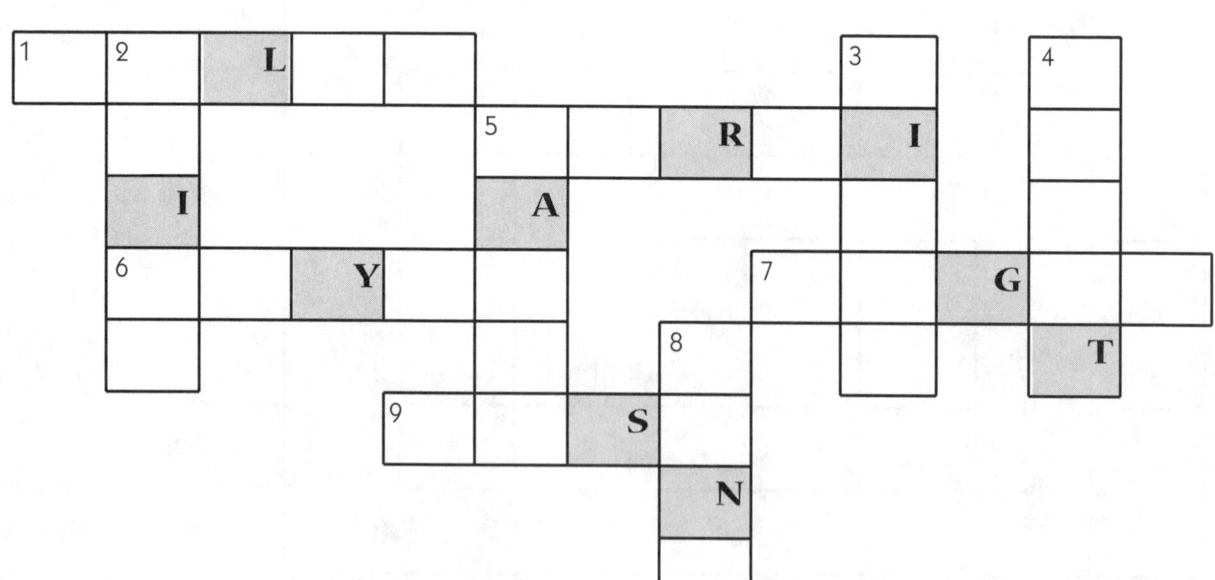

1	2	3	4	5	6	7	8	9	0

Name________________________________ Date ________

MIXED PRACTICE

What's the Difference Between Land and Sea?

Addition and subtraction review

To figure out this riddle, solve the following problems and find your answers in the code boxes below. Write the letter from each problem in the code box with the matching answer. If the answer appears in more than one code box, fill in each one with the same letter.

E	P	I	A	O
5,872 − 3,991	7,340 + 4,663	9,304 − 2,763	4,399 + 7,638	5,493 − 2,488

R	N	T	M	D
3,758 + 9,797	6,773 − 4,799	3,276 + 6,723	4,000 − 2,999	9,669 + 7,337

H	W	L	Y	S
5,803 − 4,799	4,455 + 6,677	3,090 − 1,909	2,435 + 8,876	8,429 − 7,777

Hint:
There are some extra problems and letters—don't get confused!

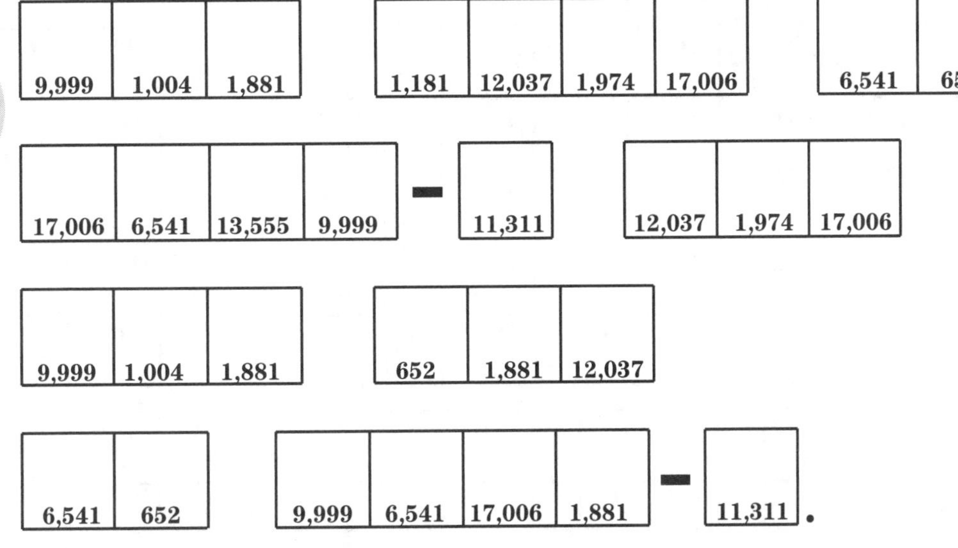

Name________________________________ Date ________ **MIXED PRACTICE**

Cross Them Out #1

Addition and subtraction review

Solve all twelve problems below. Locate and cross out each of the correct answers in the grid. Answers run horizontally, left to right. When you have finished, 35 boxes will remain. Write the remaining letters in order to reveal the answer to the following question:

What's the difference between a sailor and a bargain hunter?

1. 5,946 + 7,579

2. 6,098 − 2,409

3. 4,586 + 7,935

4. 9,930 − 8,899

5. 6,439 + 5,782

6. 9,354 − 7,839

7. 6,843 + 9,447

8. 3,289 − 2,199

9. 4,362 + 5,789

10. 9,246 − 3,172

11. 4,576 + 2,997

12. 8,422 − 5,277

O 5	N 4	F 1	E 0	W 1	T 5	O 1	E 6	S 8	A 2	I 7
E 6	R 0	B 7	A 4	L 4	S 8	D 1	G 0	T 3	P 1	T 7
H 3	E 5	S 2	E 7	R 1	F 3	R 5	S 2	U 5	A 9	S 4
T 2	H 3	G 1	U 6	E 2	P 9	D 0	E 4	O 9	T 7	H 4
E 3	W 3	O 6	K 8	N 9	R 7	S 8	T 1	F 0	S 9	E 0
E 5	E 4	S 9	W 1	E 2	F 5	G 2	D 1	T 4	H 2	E 9
W 7	E 5	L 7	B 3	S 7	A 3	C 3	N 1	M 4	V 5	L 8
E 4	R 1	O 2	Z 2	F 2	W 1	S 8	R 1	D 5	H 1	E 5

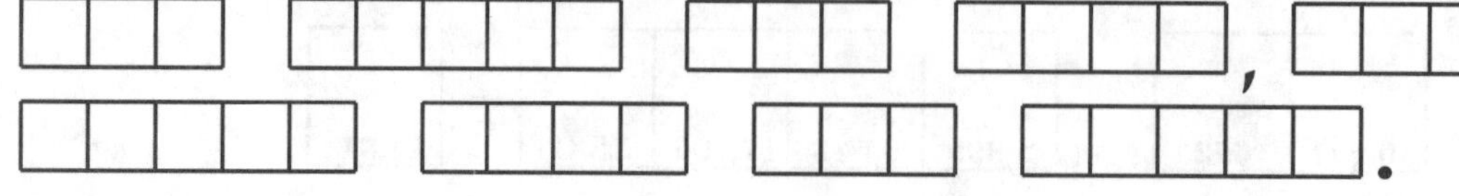

Name_______________________________ Date ________ MULTIPLICATION

Facts review

59 Errors

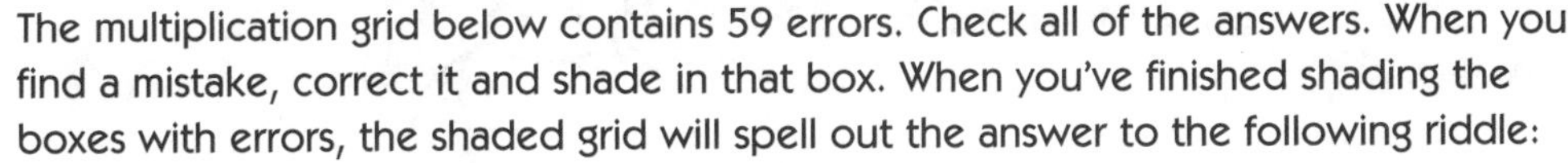

The multiplication grid below contains 59 errors. Check all of the answers. When you find a mistake, correct it and shade in that box. When you've finished shading the boxes with errors, the shaded grid will spell out the answer to the following riddle:

What is too much for one, enough for two, and nothing at all for three?

X	9	6	3	1	0	8	7	2	5	4	3	8	4	9	0	6	7	5
7	63	42	21	7	0	56	42	21	30	29	22	65	28	63	0	42	49	35
3	27	18	9	3	0	24	28	6	15	7	9	21	12	27	0	18	21	15
1	9	6	3	2	1	9	0	2	5	5	4	9	5	10	1	6	7	5
8	72	48	24	9	0	64	65	16	40	28	21	64	28	72	0	48	56	40
6	45	30	12	7	6	48	49	10	36	18	18	42	18	45	0	30	49	36
4	27	24	12	5	0	32	28	8	20	16	12	32	12	36	0	24	21	20
9	72	45	36	10	9	81	63	18	45	36	27	72	45	72	9	54	81	45
2	18	12	5	2	0	16	14	4	10	8	6	16	8	18	0	12	21	10
5	54	36	16	5	0	40	35	10	25	20	15	40	20	45	0	30	30	25

______ ______ ______ ______ ______ ______

Name________________________ Date __________ MULTIPLICATION

What a Mix-Up

Factors and products

Here are four mixed-up multiplication charts. Find the missing **factors** and **products** to complete these charts correctly.

X	5	8	2	6
3				
9		72		
4				
7				

X		4		
7			42	
		36		
2			12	
	40			24

Hint:
In the charts with missing factors, you'll notice some of the products lined up in rows or columns. Use your knowledge of common factors to help you see how these products are related.

X				5
		24	4	
	18			10
			8	
		18		

X				
		14		
	10			8
			18	
	50			

Name____ Date ________ MULTIPLICATION

Solve the Riddle

1 digit x
3 or 4 digits

Do you know what Mary had when she went out to dinner?

To figure out this riddle, solve the following problems and find your answers in the code boxes below. Write the letter from each problem in the code box with the matching answer. If the answer appears in more than one code box, fill in each one with the same letter.

K 246 × 3	**R** 4,035 × 6	**E** 319 × 9	**N** 8,007 × 5
D 7,021 × 4	**L** 9,306 × 7	**T** 999 × 8	**H** 6,210 × 2
I 5,115 × 7	**B** 8,020 × 6	**P** 583 × 9	**A** 967 × 3
M 532 × 8	**Y** 6,039 × 9	**W** 826 × 5	**O** 3,244 × 3

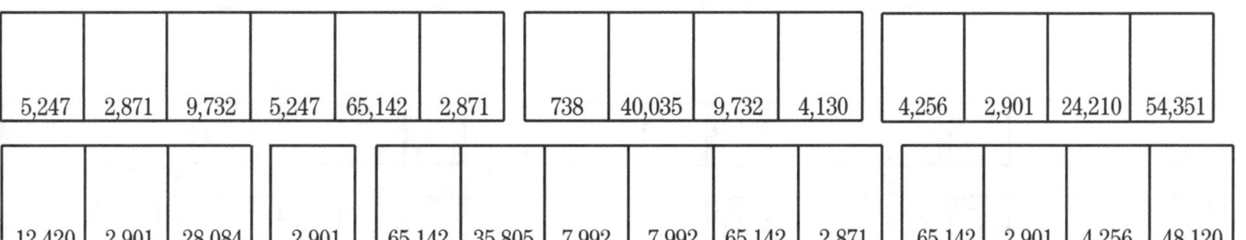

5,247 | 2,871 | 9,732 | 5,247 | 65,142 | 2,871

738 | 40,035 | 9,732 | 4,130

4,256 | 2,901 | 24,210 | 54,351

12,420 | 2,901 | 28,084

2,901

65,142 | 35,805 | 7,992 | 7,992 | 65,142 | 2,871

65,142 | 2,901 | 4,256 | 48,120 .

Name____ Date ________

MULTIPLICATION

Cross Them Out #2

1 digit x 4 digits

Solve all nine multiplication problems below. Locate and cross out each of your answers in the grid. When you have finished, 28 boxes will remain. Working horizontally, left to right, write the remaining letters in order in the empty boxes below the grid to reveal the answer to the following question:

What did the father say to his son who wanted to be a tank driver when he grew up?

1. 9,639 × 4

2. 7,092 × 3

3. 8,421 × 2

4. 5,604 × 5

5. 4,434 × 9

6. 7,638 × 8

7. 3,333 × 3

8. 8,089 × 7

9. 6,532 × 6

R 5	B 6	E 6	R 2	M 3	I 4	C 8	C 1	A 6	R 8	M 4	S 2
E 6	R 3	S 8	M 5	O 5	R 6	K 3	B 9	R 9	A 0	E 6	R 4
T 7	A 2	I 4	G 2	H 1	T 2	I 7	N 6	N 3	L 8	Y 2	W 7
B 6	R 1	I 1	M 0	S 4	O 6	N 1	T 9	S 3	T 4	A 1	N 1
T 9	R 9	I 9	M 9	D 4	I 2	N 4	I 3	N 9	G 1	S 9	B 2
Y 8	O 7	U 5	U 2	R 8	S 0	T 2	V 0	R 8	W 3	A 7	Y 5

☐ ☐☐☐☐☐☐☐☐☐ ☐☐☐'☐

☐☐☐☐☐ ☐☐ ☐☐☐☐ ☐☐☐.

Name________________________________ Date ________ **MULTIPLICATION**

Match It #1

2 digits x 2 digits

Use multiplication to solve the problems below, then locate each correct answer in the column on the right. Use a ruler or a straightedge to draw a line from the question to the answer (dot to dot). Your line will pass through a number and a letter. The number tells you where to write your letter in the code boxes to answer the riddle below.

1. 54 x 31 ●		● 4,508
2. 29 x 84 ●		● 2,378
3. 32 x 23 ●		● 2,961
4. 49 x 92 ●		● 1,152
5. 66 x 40 ●		● 2,640
6. 35 x 72 ●		● 736
7. 63 x 47 ●		● 2,166
8. 13 x 62 ●		● 1,674
9. 48 x 24 ●		● 3,528
10. 57 x 38 ●		● 806
11. 82 x 29 ●		● 2,436
12. 72 x 49 ●		● 2,520

A
3 K O
A 9 5 6
12 M R
R
10 O 8
11 4
2
C N 7 1
O
I

Where does a frog change its clothes?

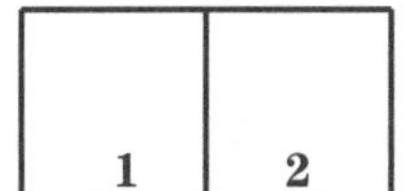
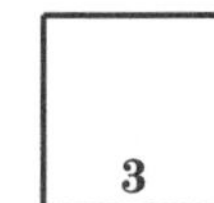

4	5	6	7	8

9	10	11	12

Name____________________ Date ________

MULTIPLICATION

2 digits x 2 digits

Secret Code Time

Why did Godzilla eat Tokyo instead of Rome?

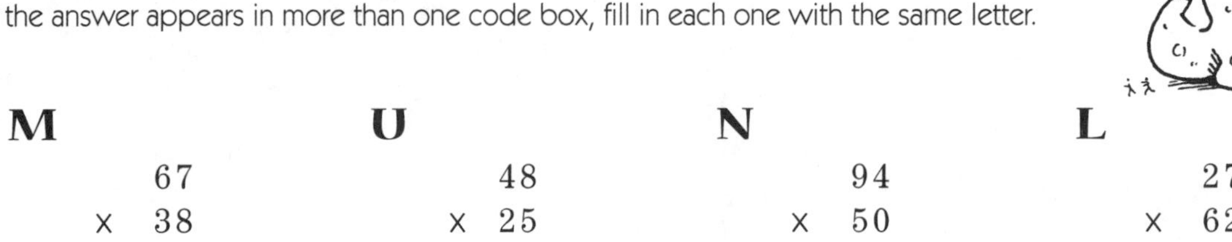

To figure out this riddle, solve the following problems and find your answers in the code boxes below. Write the letter from each problem in the code box with the matching answer. If the answer appears in more than one code box, fill in each one with the same letter.

M	U	N	L
67 × 38	48 × 25	94 × 50	27 × 62

W	T	D	O
53 × 35	79 × 29	58 × 34	41 × 79

I	J	E	F
55 × 84	47 × 24	62 × 37	90 × 30

R	S	A	H
24 × 25	92 × 38	47 × 96	52 × 87

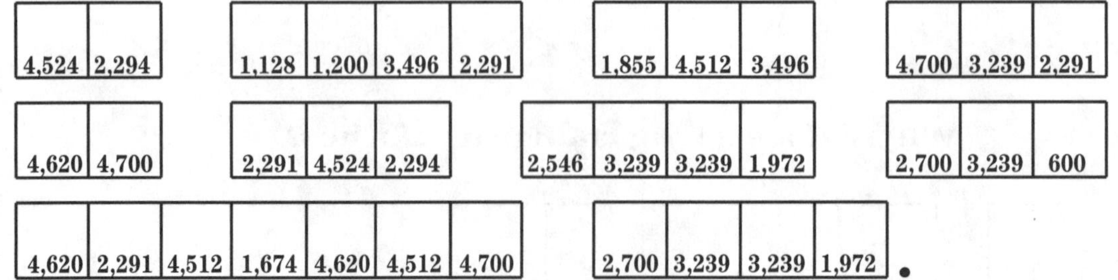

[4,524] [2,294]   [1,128] [1,200] [3,496] [2,291]   [1,855] [4,512] [3,496]   [4,700] [3,239] [2,291]

[4,620] [4,700]   [2,291] [4,524] [2,294]   [2,546] [3,239] [3,239] [1,972]   [2,700] [3,239] [600]

[4,620] [2,291] [4,512] [1,674] [4,620] [4,512] [4,700]   [2,700] [3,239] [3,239] [1,972].

Name________________________________ Date ________ **MULTIPLICATION**

2 digits x 3 digits

Monster Mystery

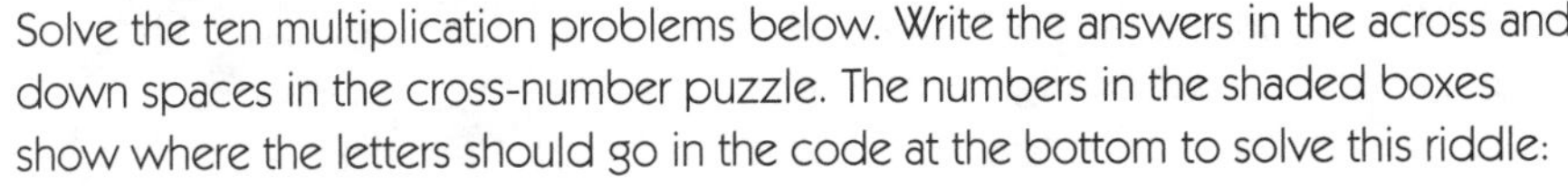

Solve the ten multiplication problems below. Write the answers in the across and down spaces in the cross-number puzzle. The numbers in the shaded boxes show where the letters should go in the code at the bottom to solve this riddle:

What did the hungry monster eat after the dentist pulled its tooth?

ACROSS

1. 384 x 64	**5.** 908 x 62	**6.** 787 x 78	**8.** 473 x 64	**9.** 669 x 66

DOWN

1. 586 x 37	**2.** 824 x 93	**3.** 960 x 28	**4.** 168 x 75	**7.** 339 x 45

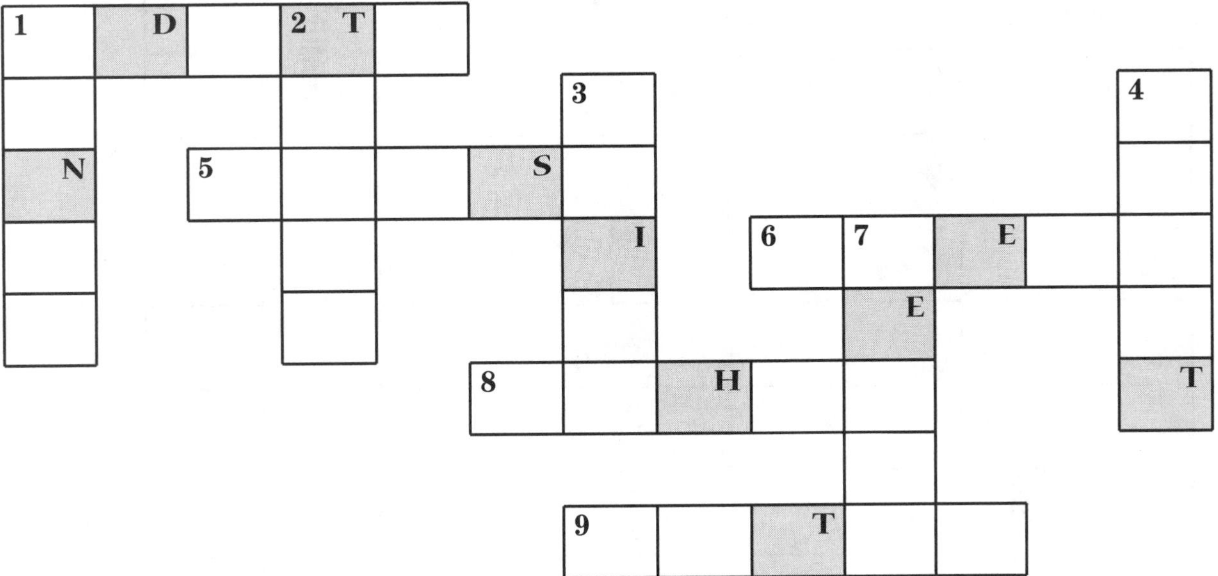

1	2	3

4	5	6	7	8	9	0

Name_______________________________ Date _________ MULTIPLICATION

Last Number–First Number #2

2 digits x 3 digits

Solve the following multiplication problems. Write your answers in the winding puzzle below. **Note: The last digit of each answer becomes the first digit of the next answer.** Be sure to follow the arrows as you fill in the boxes, because you will have to write the following answers backward: numbers 5, 6, 7, 8, 11, and 12. After you've finished the puzzle, look at the numbers you've written in the shaded boxes. Each number shows where the letter in that box should go in the code at the bottom to answer this riddle:

What does the announcer say to start a flea race?

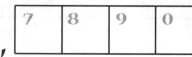

1.	2.	3.	4.	5.	6.
467 x 39	529 x 64	937 x 65	833 x 62	724 x 83	437 x 53

7.	8.	9.	10.	11.	12.
337 x 39	972 x 33	861 x 74	511 x 83	947 x 42	827 x 53

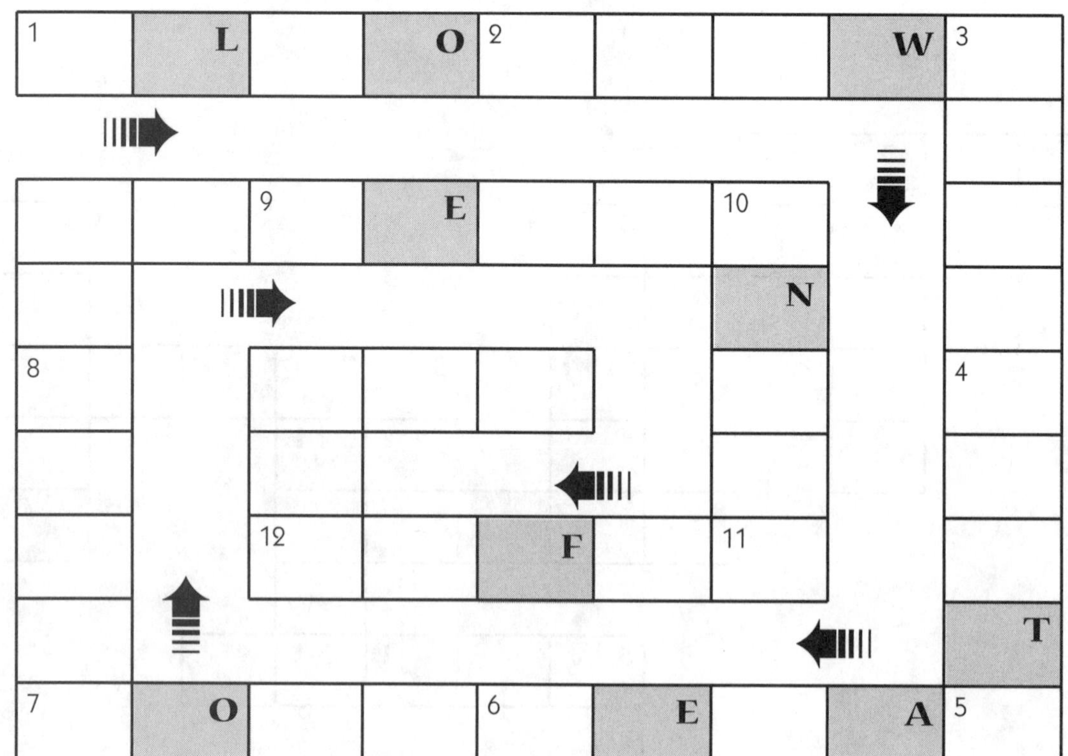

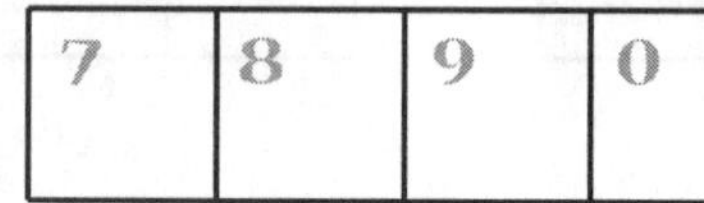

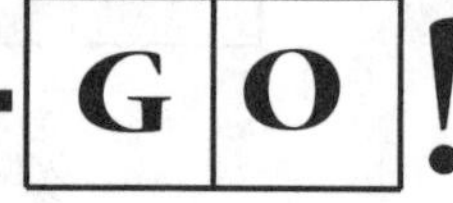

Name______________________________ Date ________ MIXED PRACTICE

Equal Values #1

Addition, subtraction, and multiplication review

What's the best way to double your money?

Solve all the problems in both sets of boxes. Each answer in the top boxes matches an answer in the bottom boxes. Discover the answer to the question above by writing each word from the top set of boxes in the box below with the matching answer. One example has been done for you.

82 x 3= 246 **IF**	25 x 5= **BUT**	44 x 6= **IT**	74 x 3= **IT**	22 x 8= **FIND**
18 x 8= **IT**	33 x 3= **IF**	51 x 2= **AGAIN**	69 x 7= **YOU**	84 x 5= **BILL**
58 x 5= **FOLD**	30 x 3= **DOUBLE**	80 x 3= **YOU'LL**	16 x 4= **YOU**	70 x 3= **INCREASES**
24 x 9= **UP**	19 x 5= **OPEN**	48 x 1= **THE**	78 x 2= **YOU**	15 x 3= **FIVE-DOLLAR**

11 x 9= ________	8 x 8= ________	29 x 10= ________	12 x 4= ________	5 x 9= ________
60 x 7= ________,	500 – 17= ________	45 x 2= ________	259 – 37= ________.	150 – 25= ________
41 x 6= 246 if	39 x 4= ________	70 + 25= ________	12 x 12= ________	72 x 3= ________
17 x 6= ________,	60 x 4= ________	44 x 4= ________	66 x 4= ________	42 x 5= ________.

Name________________________ Date ________

DIVISION

1-digit divisor/ 3- or 4- digit quotient

Did You Hear? Riddles

Did you hear . . .

about your muscles? NEVER MIND —

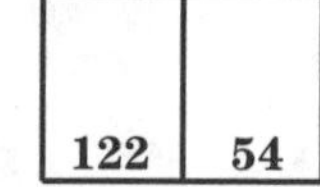

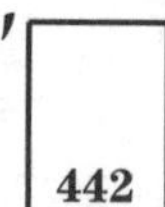

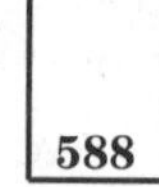

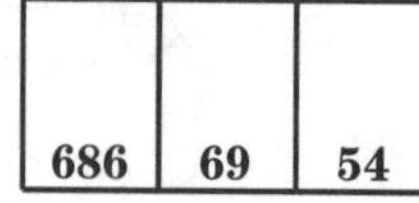

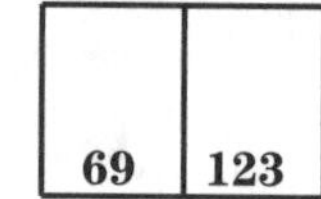

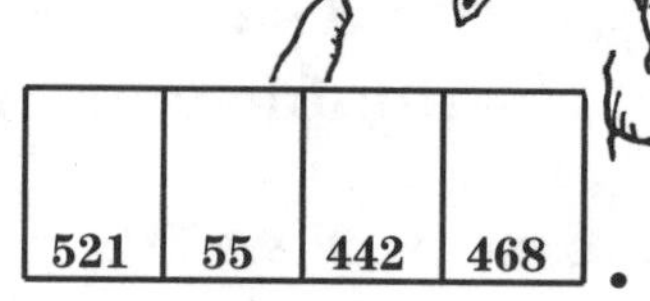

about the rotten pudding? NEVER MIND —

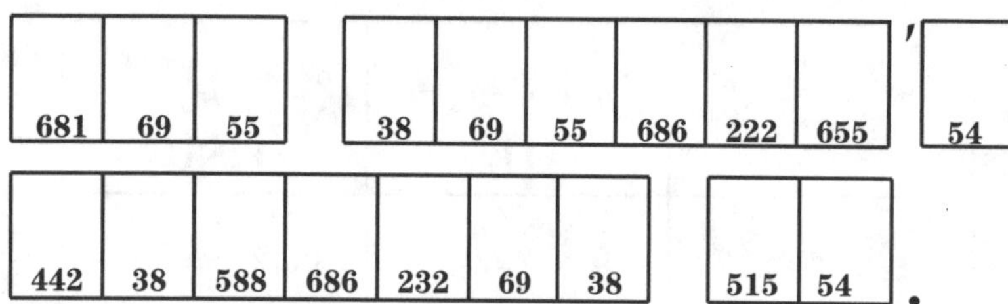

To decode these jokes, complete the division problems below and locate the answers in the code boxes below the riddles. Write the letter from the problem above the matching answer in each code box. If the answer appears in more than one code box, fill in each one with the same letter.

W 5) 190	**O** 7) 483	**D** 4) 888	**L** 2) 1,372
T 8) 432	**M** 6) 3,126	**Y** 9) 6,129	**H** 3) 1,404
S 6) 2,652	**A** 2) 1,176	**F** 9) 1,107	**U** 5) 275
N 3) 1,965	**I** 7) 3,605	**L** 4) 928	**I** 8) 976

Name______________________ Date __________

DIVISION

Remainders

1-digit divisor/
3-digit quotient

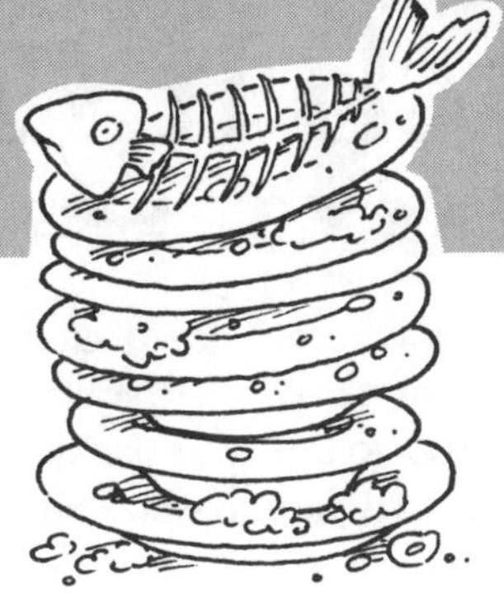

Solve the division problems below. Each answer has a remainder. Write the remainder **in words** in the puzzle below. The clue above the problem tells you where the remainder should go.

1 ACROSS	1 DOWN	2 ACROSS	2 DOWN
$9\overline{)708}$	$8\overline{)743}$	$7\overline{)341}$	$5\overline{)249}$

3 ACROSS	3 DOWN	4 DOWN	5 ACROSS
$8\overline{)555}$	$5\overline{)452}$	$9\overline{)611}$	$8\overline{)713}$

6 ACROSS	7 ACROSS	7 DOWN	8 DOWN
$5\overline{)192}$	$7\overline{)675}$	$9\overline{)587}$	$8\overline{)711}$

Name________________________________ Date __________

Match It #2

1-digit divisor/ 4-digit quotient

Use division to solve the problems below, then locate each correct answer in the column on the right. Use a ruler or a straightedge to draw a line from the question to the answer (dot to dot). Your line will pass through a number and a letter. The number tells you where to write your letter in the code boxes to answer the riddle below.

1. 5,247 ÷ 9 ●		● 949
2. 1,230 ÷ 5 ●	F	● 560
3. 2,712 ÷ 8 ●	3 8 L	● 226
4. 2,847 ÷ 3 ●	O N 7	● 415
5. 2,658 ÷ 6 ●	R E 5 P	● 339
6. 818 ÷ 2 ●	9 2	● 443
7. 3,920 ÷ 7 ●	Y T	● 764
8. 1,200 ÷ 4 ●	O O 11 4 6 12	● 793
9. 6,112 ÷ 8 ●		● 583
10. 1,356 ÷ 6 ●	1 M 10	● 300
11. 7,137 ÷ 9 ●		● 409
12. 2,075 ÷ 5 ●		● 246

What do you give a seasick elephant?

1	2	3	4	5	6

7	8

9	10	11	12

Name______________________________ Date __________

DIVISION

99s

2-digit divisor/
4-digit quotient

The divisor in all nine of the following problems is 99. The multiples of 99, from 0 to 9, are listed in the box below. Check your final answer against the correct answers in the answer box.

99 x 0	99 x 1	99 x 2	99 x 3	99 x 4	99 x 5	99 x 6	99 x 7	99 x 8	99 x 9
0	99	198	297	396	495	594	693	792	891

1. $99\overline{)2{,}307}$ **2.** $99\overline{)5{,}592}$ **3.** $99\overline{)7{,}060}$

4. $99\overline{)6{,}378}$ **5.** $99\overline{)3{,}680}$ **6.** $99\overline{)8{,}764}$

7. $99\overline{)4{,}890}$ **8.** $99\overline{)5{,}666}$ **9.** $99\overline{)7{,}548}$

Hint:
Some problems have remainders that may be longer than the two digit remainders given in the answer boxes.

ANSWER BOX

37 r 17	41 r 14	88 r 52	71 r 31
49 r 39	23 r 30	64 r 42	57 r 23
56 r 48	62 r 26	76 r 24	39 r 39

Name________________________________ Date __________

DIVISION

MORE Did You Hear? Riddles

2-digit divisor/
4-digit quotient

Did you hear . . .

about the rotten food? NEVER MIND—

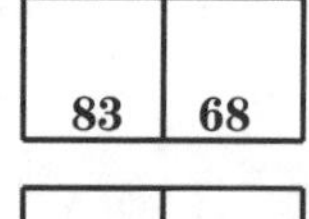
83 | 68

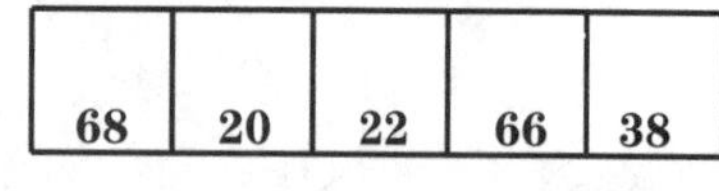
68 | 20 | 22 | 66 | 38

43 | 40   38 | 68 | 41 | 43 | 75 | 35 | 86 .

about the chef who dropped the egg? NEVER MIND—

83 | 68   35 | 22 | 75 | 39 | 80 | 38   43 | 21   20 | 13 .

To decode these jokes, complete the division problems below and locate the answers in the code boxes below the riddles. Write the letter from the problem above the matching answer in each code box. If the answer appears in more than one code box, fill in each one with the same letter.

P 64) 832

A 27) 2,025

T 70) 4,760

H 15) 1,290

R 48) 1,056

O 98) 4,018

U 20) 400

K 43) 3,440

Y 52) 2,080

I 22) 1,826

M 42) 1,806

C 11) 385

S 74) 2,812

C 84) 3,276

E 77) 1,617

N 55) 3,630

Name______________________________ Date ________ MIXED PRACTICE

Follow the Arrows #1

Addition, subtraction, multiplication, and division review

Begin at the ▶. Solve the addition problem and write your answer in the box directly below it. Follow the arrow to the next box and copy your answer from the first box. Solve the next problem, follow the arrow, and copy your new answer in the next open box. Continue to solve the problems, copying each answer into the next box indicated by the arrow. When you've finished the puzzle correctly, your final answer should be the exact number needed to solve the final problem. Go on to the second puzzle and follow the same steps you used to work your way through the first one!

▶ 5,934
2,202
7,864
2,135
+ 796

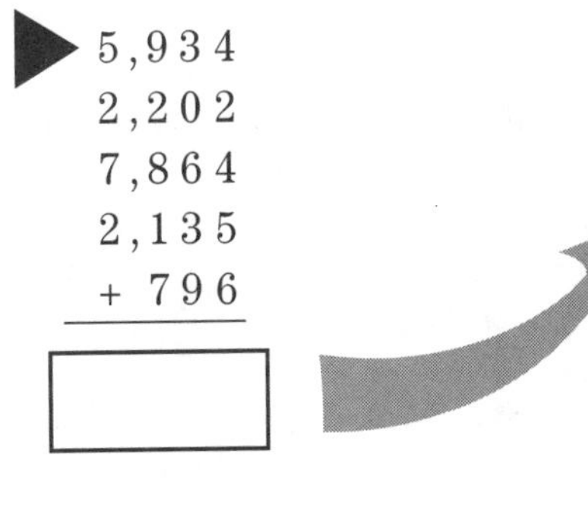

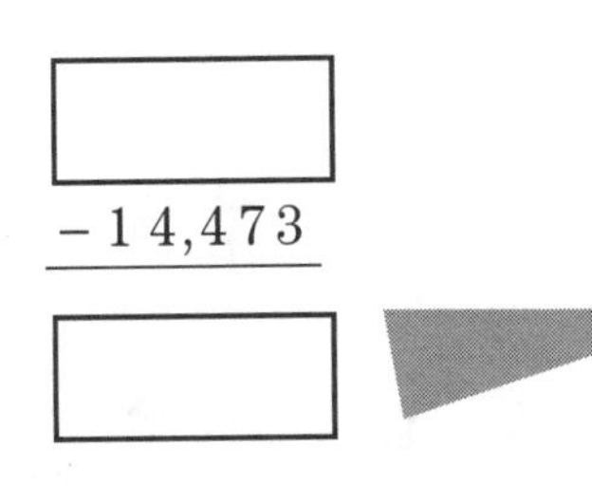

− 14,473

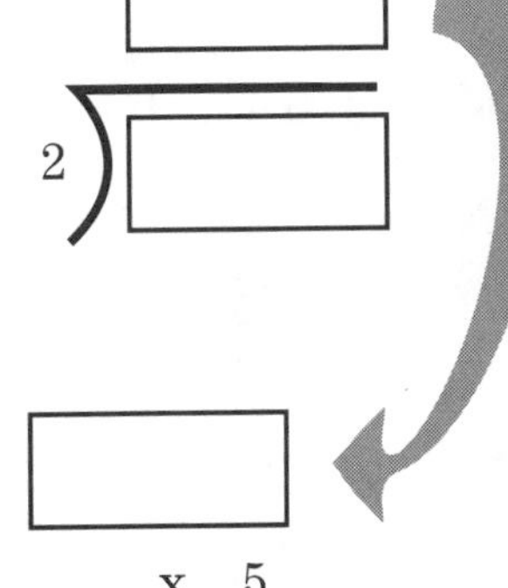

2) ☐

x 5

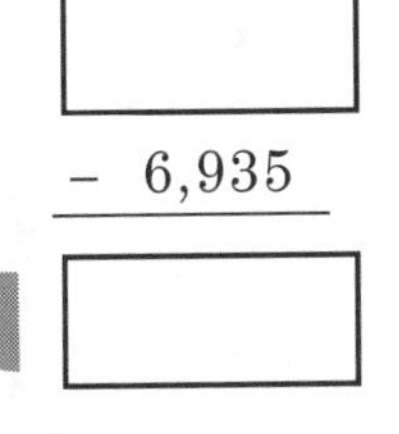

− 6,935

842

5) ☐

Hint:
As you work through these problems, check your answers by using the reverse operation.
For example: 54 x 3 = 162
check: 162 ÷ 3 = 54

▶ 6,489
7,351
4,007
+ 6,397

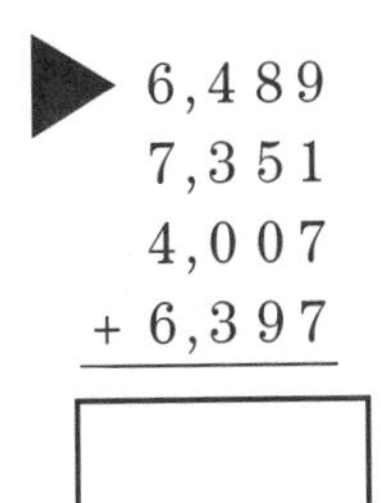

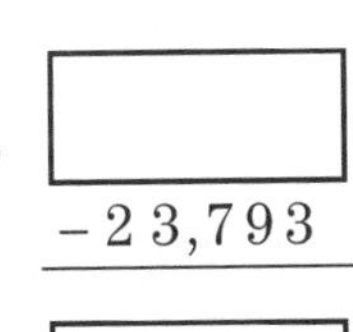

− 23,793

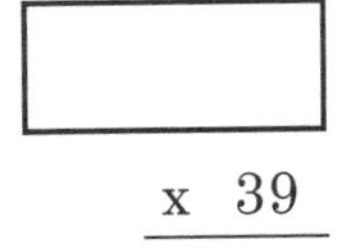

x 39

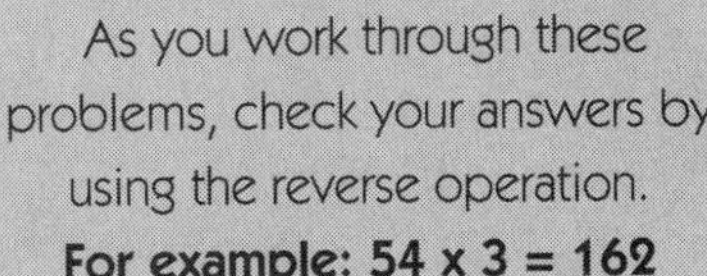

− 12,375

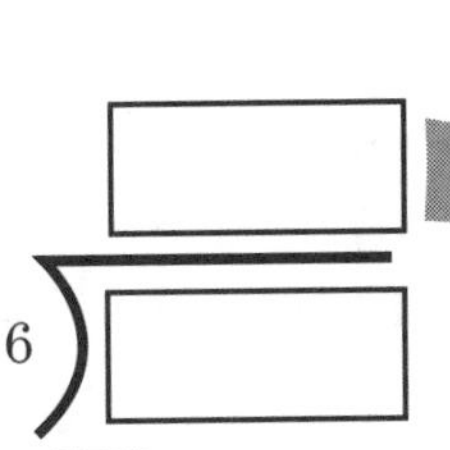

6) ☐

x 54

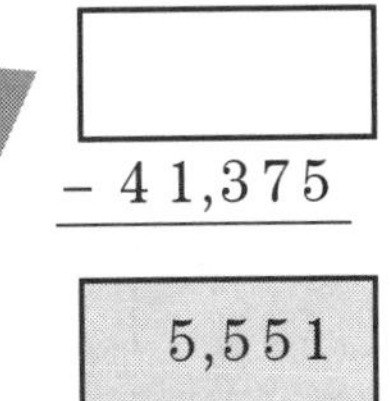

− 41,375

5,551

Name______________________________ Date __________

MIXED PRACTICE

Addition, subtraction, multiplication, and division review

Solve each problem by working from left to right. When you finish a problem, locate the answer in a box below, then write the letter above the answer. If the answer appears in more than one box, fill in each one with the same letter.

Take **48**	→ Multiply by **8**	→ Subtract **64**	→ Divide **4**	=	______	= **N**
Take **408**	→ Add **72**	→ Divide by **5**	→ Subtract **19**	=	______	= **A**
Take **937**	→ Subtract **83**	→ Divide by **7**	→ Multiply by **9**	=	______	= **D**
Take **396**	→ Divide by **6**	→ Add **48**	→ Subtract **78**	=	______	= **S**
Take **407**	→ Add **49**	→ Divide by **4**	→ Subtract **70**	=	______	= **L**
Take **596**	→ Multiply by **9**	→ Subtract **64**	→ Divide by **5**	=	______	= **B**
Take **486**	→ Divide by **6**	→ Add **40**	→ Multiply by **7**	=	______	= **G**
Take **784**	→ Subtract **229**	→ Divide by **5**	→ Add **72**	=	______	= **U**
Take **420**	→ Add **777**	→ Subtract **42**	→ Divide by **5**	=	______	= **Y**
Take **92**	→ Multiply by **8**	→ Subtract **1**	→ Divide by **7**	=	______	= **O**

What strange children live in the ocean?

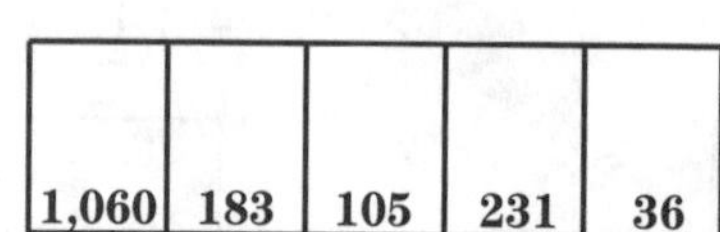

1,060	183	105	231	36

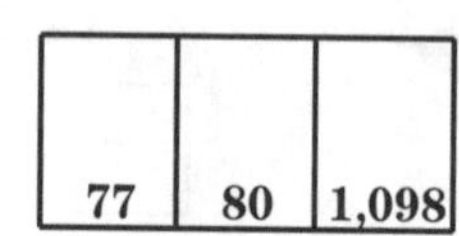

77	80	1,098

847	183	44	44	36

Name________________________ Date ________

MIXED PRACTICE

Shapely Math #1

Addition, subtraction, multiplication, and division review

Study the shapes in equations 1–6. Each shape has only one match in the number grids. Use the shapes to fill in the missing numbers in the equations. Solve each number sentence. Check your answers against the scrambled answers in the Answer Box.

63	87	35
48	22	74
57	91	46

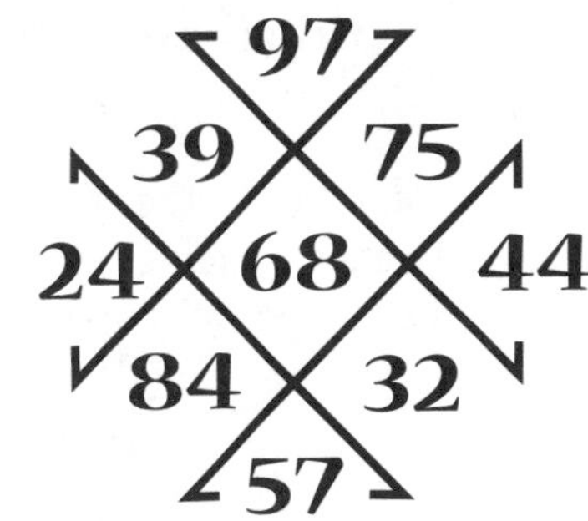

1. (☐ x 44) ÷ (68 - ☐) = ________

2. (☐ x ☐) ÷ (☐ - ☐) = ________

3. (☐ x ☐) ÷ (☐ - ☐) = ________

4. (☐ x ☐) ÷ (☐ - ☐) = ________

5. (☐ x ☐) ÷ (☐ - ☐) = ________

6. (☐ x ☐) ÷ (☐ - ☐) = ________

ANSWER BOX

394 r 4	507	461 r 4
768	550	192
422 r 2	35 r 40	1323

Name______________________ Date ________

ORDER OF OPERATIONS

Addition and multiplication

Elephant Trivia

Why did the elephant cross the road?

Solve the problems below. Locate your answer in the code boxes and write the letter from the matching problem above it. If the answer appears in more than one box, fill in each one with the same letter.

J = (5 x 6) + (6 x 3) + (4 x 9) = 

L = (2 x 8) + (8 x 6) + (7 x 3) = 

O = (5 x 7) + (6 x 9) + (3 x 5) = 

D = (3 x 8) + (6 x 4) + (2 x 12) = 

I = (4 x 8) + (9 x 5) + (9 x 4) = 

T = (6 x 6) + (4 x 7) + (3 x 9) = 

S = (9 x 7) + (9 x 6) + (8 x 6) = 

W = (4 x 9) + (9 x 9) + (6 x 7) = 

K = (1 x 9) + (7 x 8) + (2 x 8) = 

E = (5 x 5) + (5 x 7) + (6 x 5) = 

N = (4 x 8) + (9 x 0) + (8 x 4) = 

H = (3 x 3) + (4 x 4) + (5 x 5) = 

A = (3 x 7) + (4 x 7) + (7 x 9) = 

R = (8 x 8) + (7 x 7) + (6 x 6) = 

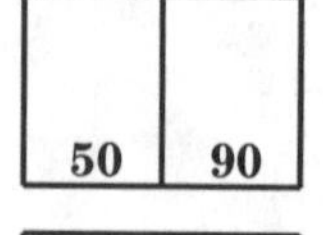

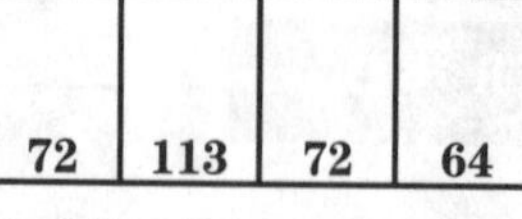

'
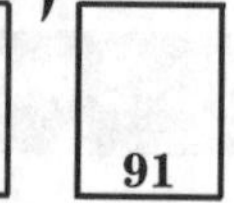

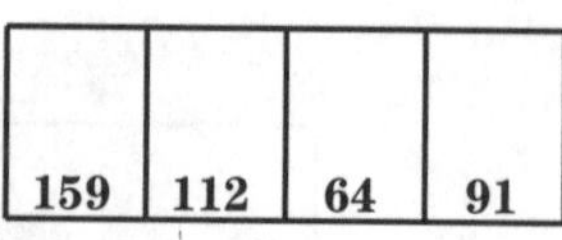

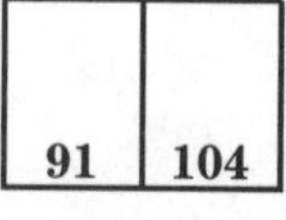

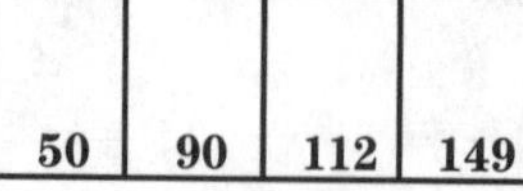

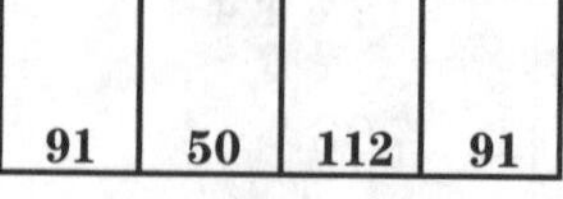

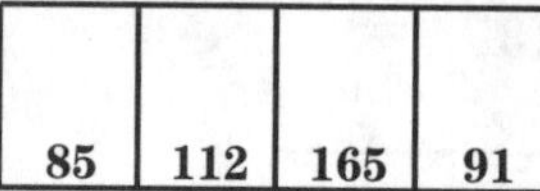

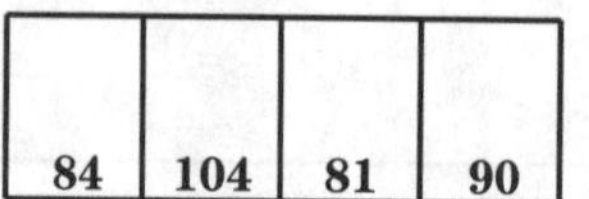

.

Name________________________________ Date ______

ORDER OF OPERATIONS

Addition and multiplication

Riddle Time

What has 500 teeth and says "Beware of Dog"?

Solve the problems below. Locate your answer in the code boxes and write the letter from the matching problem above it. If the answer appears in more than one box, fill in each one with the same letter.

(5 x 9) + 3 = **T**	**T** =	(**K** x 7) + 5 = 54	**K** =
(3 x 9) + 7 = **G**	**G** =	(5 x 5) + 6 = **C**	**C** =
(7 x 4) + 8 = **E**	**E** =	(**H** x 8) + 3 = 75	**H** =
(**A** x 6) + 4 = 40	**A** =	(4 x 8) + 8 = **N**	**N** =
(8 x 8) + 4 = **F**	**F** =	(**S** x 6) + 5 = 53	**S** =
(**W** x 9) + 8 = 53	**W** =	(4 x 4) + 9 = **P**	**P** =
(6 x 4) + 9 = **I**	**I** =	(9 x 2) + 8 = **O**	**O** =

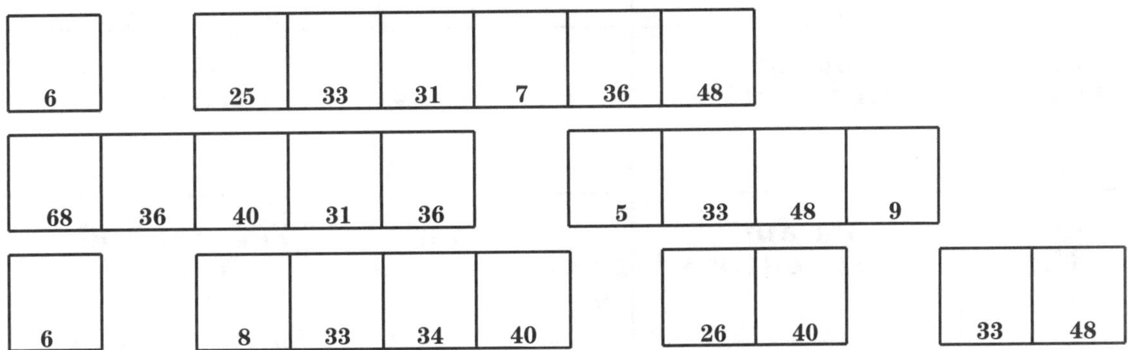

Name____________________ Date ________ FRACTIONS

Equal Values #2

Renaming and reducing fractions

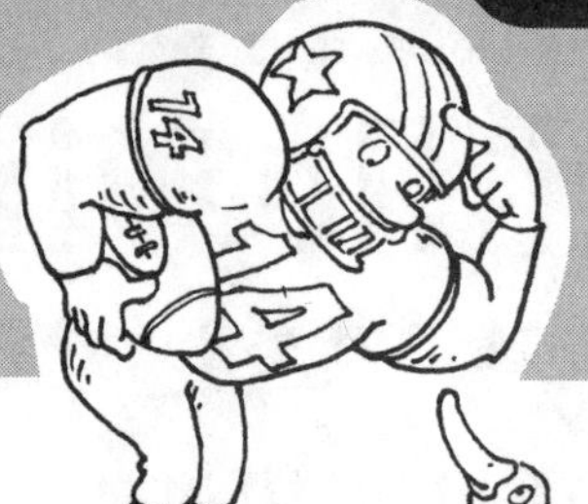

What is the difference between a football player and a duck?

Change the improper fractions in the top boxes to mixed numerals in their simplest form. Then match each answer in the top boxes to an equivalent mixed numeral, expressed in words, in the bottom boxes. Discover the answer to the question above by writing each word from the top set of boxes in the box below with the matching answer. One example has been done for you.

$\frac{5}{3} =$ DUCK	$\frac{14}{10} = 1\frac{4}{10} = 1\frac{2}{5}$ A	$\frac{9}{6} =$ PUDDLE	$\frac{8}{5} =$ BUT
$\frac{13}{8} =$ HUDDLE	$\frac{17}{14} =$ A	$\frac{7}{4} =$ PLAYER	$\frac{17}{12} =$ IN
$\frac{12}{7} =$ IN	$\frac{10}{8} =$ FOOTBALL	$\frac{9}{4} =$ FOUND	$\frac{11}{6} =$ IS
$\frac{9}{7} =$ A	$\frac{5}{2} =$ A	$\frac{12}{9} =$ IS	$\frac{13}{12} =$ FOUND

one and two fifths = A	one and one fourth = ______	one and three fourths = ______	one and one third = ______
one and one twelfth = ______	one and five sevenths = ______	two and one half = ______	one and five eighths = ______ ,
one and three fifths = ______	one and two sevenths = ______	one and two thirds = ______	one and five sixths = ______
two and one fourth = ______	one and five twelfths = ______	one and three fourteenths = ______	one and one half = ______ .

Name________________________ Date ________ **FRACTIONS**

A Sharp Riddle

Addition with unlike denominators

If two vampires had a race, who would win?

To figure out this riddle, solve the following problems and find your answers in the code boxes below. Remember to reduce fractions when necessary. Write the letter from each problem in the code box with the matching answer. If the answer appears in more than one code box, fill in each one with the same letter.

D $\frac{2}{3} + \frac{2}{4} =$	**E** $\frac{4}{6} - \frac{1}{3} =$	**F** $\frac{3}{4} - \frac{2}{5} =$	**S** $\frac{1}{6} + \frac{3}{9} =$
T $\frac{4}{5} - \frac{1}{2} =$	**O** $\frac{3}{2} + \frac{2}{3} =$	**R** $\frac{2}{3} + \frac{5}{8} =$	**Y** $\frac{5}{6} - \frac{3}{5} =$
I $\frac{3}{9} + \frac{1}{2} =$	**H** $\frac{3}{4} - \frac{5}{10} =$	**L** $\frac{2}{4} + \frac{5}{6} =$	**C** $\frac{5}{6} - \frac{3}{8} =$
U $\frac{4}{5} - \frac{2}{3} =$	**K** $\frac{3}{4} + \frac{2}{3} =$	**W** $\frac{6}{7} - \frac{2}{3} =$	**N** $\frac{1}{2} + \frac{3}{7} =$

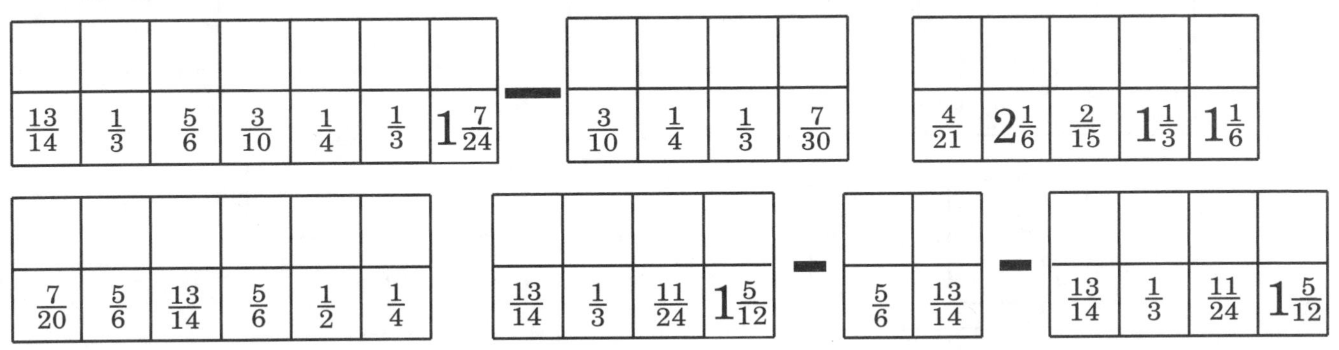

$\frac{13}{14}$ $\frac{1}{3}$ $\frac{5}{6}$ $\frac{3}{10}$ $\frac{1}{4}$ $\frac{1}{3}$ $1\frac{7}{24}$ – $\frac{3}{10}$ $\frac{1}{4}$ $\frac{1}{3}$ $\frac{7}{30}$ $\frac{4}{21}$ $2\frac{1}{6}$ $\frac{2}{15}$ $1\frac{1}{3}$ $1\frac{1}{6}$

$\frac{7}{20}$ $\frac{5}{6}$ $\frac{13}{14}$ $\frac{5}{6}$ $\frac{1}{2}$ $\frac{1}{4}$ $\frac{13}{14}$ $\frac{1}{3}$ $\frac{11}{24}$ $1\frac{5}{12}$ – $\frac{5}{6}$ $\frac{13}{14}$ – $\frac{13}{14}$ $\frac{1}{3}$ $\frac{11}{24}$ $1\frac{5}{12}$.

Name________________________________ Date __________

Order of operations

Wrestle the Code

What did the wrestler say when he sat down to eat at the buffet?

Solve the problems below. Remember to reduce fractions when necessary. Locate your answer in the code boxes and write the letter from the matching problem above it. If the answer appears in more than one box, fill in each one with the same letter.

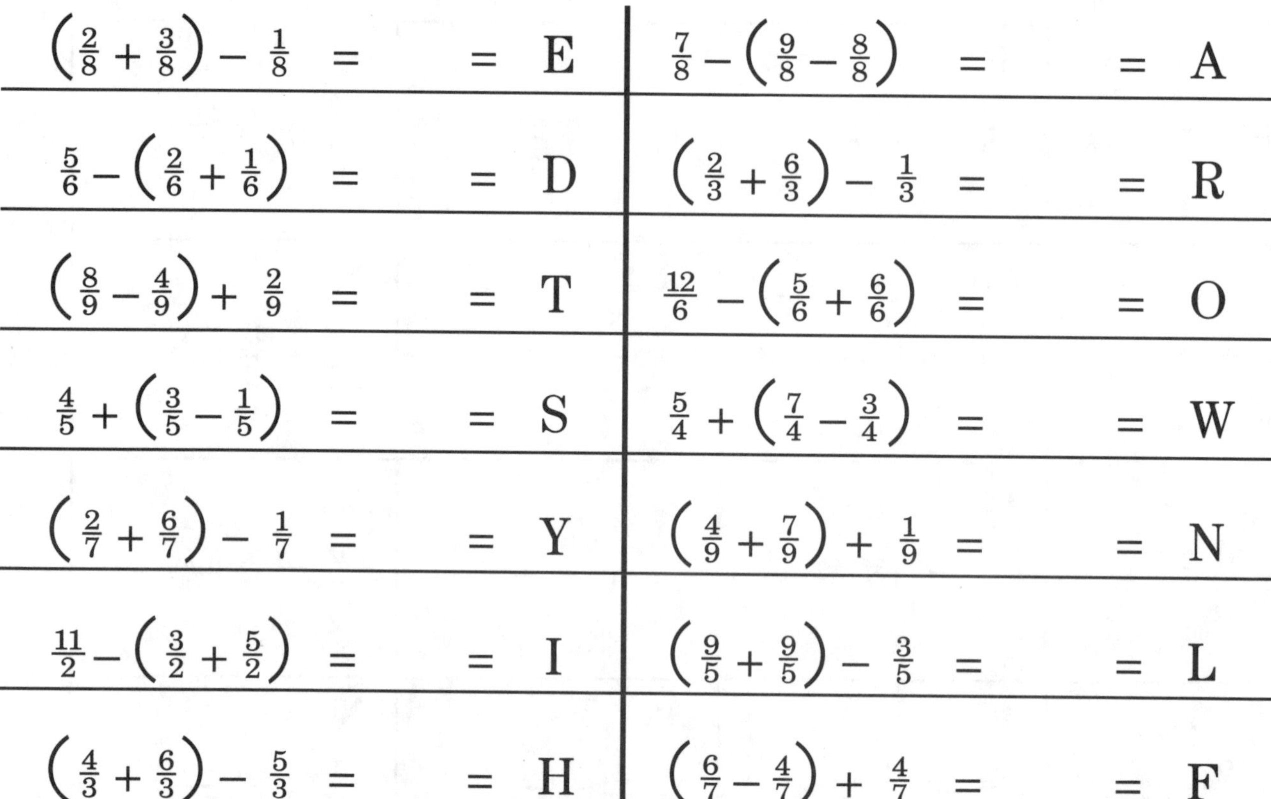

$\left(\frac{2}{8} + \frac{3}{8}\right) - \frac{1}{8} = ___ = $ E

$\frac{5}{6} - \left(\frac{2}{6} + \frac{1}{6}\right) = ___ = $ D

$\left(\frac{8}{9} - \frac{4}{9}\right) + \frac{2}{9} = ___ = $ T

$\frac{4}{5} + \left(\frac{3}{5} - \frac{1}{5}\right) = ___ = $ S

$\left(\frac{2}{7} + \frac{6}{7}\right) - \frac{1}{7} = ___ = $ Y

$\frac{11}{2} - \left(\frac{3}{2} + \frac{5}{2}\right) = ___ = $ I

$\left(\frac{4}{3} + \frac{6}{3}\right) - \frac{5}{3} = ___ = $ H

$\frac{7}{8} - \left(\frac{9}{8} - \frac{8}{8}\right) = ___ = $ A

$\left(\frac{2}{3} + \frac{6}{3}\right) - \frac{1}{3} = ___ = $ R

$\frac{12}{6} - \left(\frac{5}{6} + \frac{6}{6}\right) = ___ = $ O

$\frac{5}{4} + \left(\frac{7}{4} - \frac{3}{4}\right) = ___ = $ W

$\left(\frac{4}{9} + \frac{7}{9}\right) + \frac{1}{9} = ___ = $ N

$\left(\frac{9}{5} + \frac{9}{5}\right) - \frac{3}{5} = ___ = $ L

$\left(\frac{6}{7} - \frac{4}{7}\right) + \frac{4}{7} = ___ = $ F

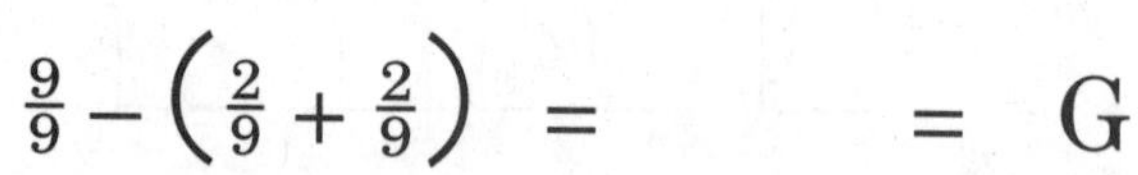

$\frac{9}{9} - \left(\frac{2}{9} + \frac{2}{9}\right) = ___ = $ G

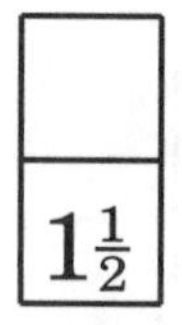

$1\frac{1}{2}$

$2\frac{1}{3}$	$\frac{1}{2}$	$\frac{3}{4}$	3	3	1

$\frac{1}{3}$	$\frac{1}{6}$	$1\frac{1}{3}$

'

$\frac{2}{3}$

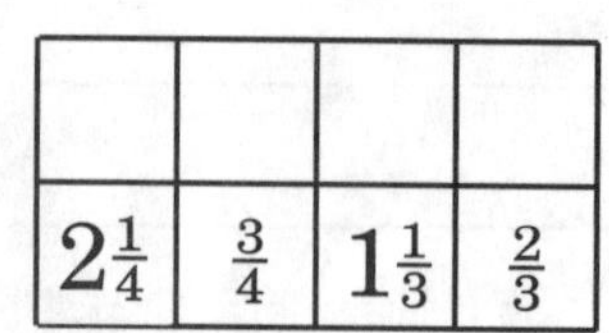

$2\frac{1}{4}$	$\frac{3}{4}$	$1\frac{1}{3}$	$\frac{2}{3}$

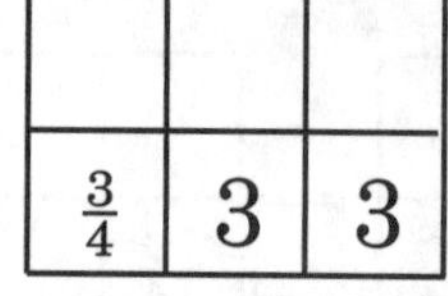

$\frac{3}{4}$	3	3

$\frac{2}{3}$	$1\frac{2}{3}$	$1\frac{1}{2}$	$1\frac{1}{5}$

$\frac{6}{7}$	$\frac{1}{6}$	$\frac{1}{6}$	$\frac{1}{3}$

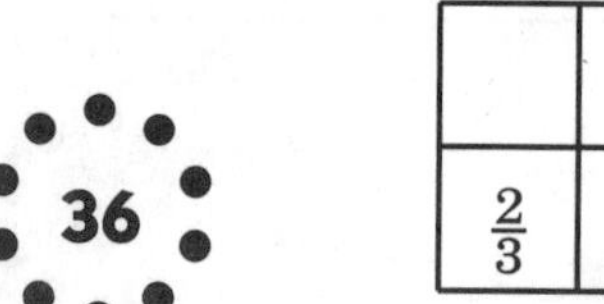

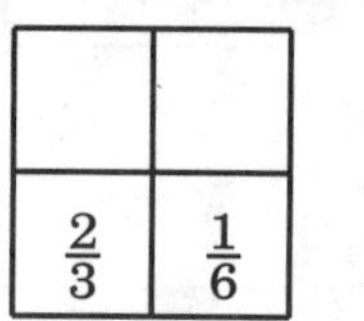

$\frac{2}{3}$	$\frac{1}{6}$

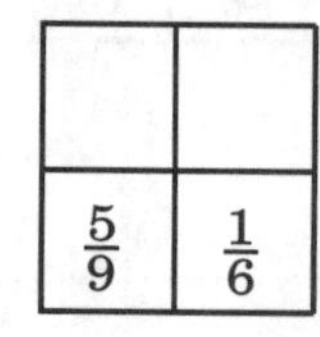

$\frac{5}{9}$	$\frac{1}{6}$

$\frac{2}{3}$	$\frac{1}{6}$

$2\frac{1}{4}$	$\frac{3}{4}$	$1\frac{1}{2}$	$1\frac{1}{5}$	$\frac{2}{3}$

.

Name________________________ Date ______ DECIMALS

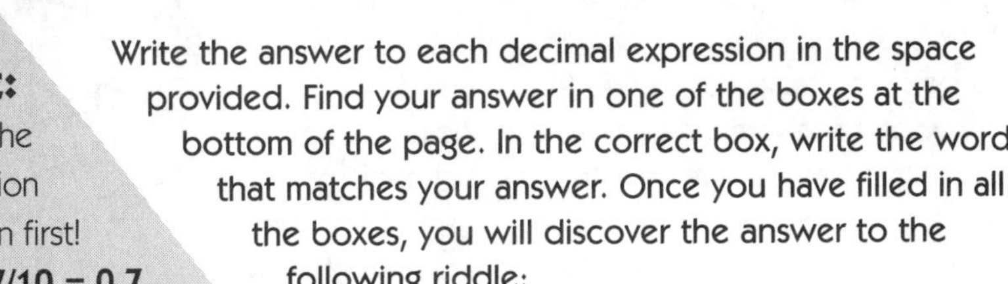

Decimal Match

Equivalent fractions and decimals

Hint: Write the expression as a fraction first! **For example: 7/10 = 0.7**

Write the answer to each decimal expression in the space provided. Find your answer in one of the boxes at the bottom of the page. In the correct box, write the word that matches your answer. Once you have filled in all the boxes, you will discover the answer to the following riddle:

How do we know football referees are happy?

1. Three tenths = ________ = ________ = **Happy**
2. Thirteen and one thousandth = ________ = ________ = **Know**
3. Four and four hundredths = ________ = ________ = **Are**
4. Seven and fifteen thousandths = ________ = ________ = **Always**
5. Thirteen and one hundredth = ________ = ________ = **While**
6. Four and four thousandths = ________ = ________ = **They**
7. Three hundredths = ________ = ________ = **Referees**
8. Thirteen and one tenth = ________ = ________ = **They**
9. Four and forty thousandths = ________ = ________ = **We**
10. Thirteen and ten hundredths = ________ = ________ = **Work**
11. Four and four tenths = ________ = ________ = **Because**
12. Seven and fifteen hundredths = ________ = ________ = **Whistle**

4.040	13.001	0.03	4.04
0.3	4.4	4.004	7.015
7.15	13.01	13.1	13.10

Name________________________ Date __________

Mixed practice

Follow the Arrows #2

THIS WAY

THAT WAY

Begin at the ★. Solve the addition problem and write your answer in the box directly below it. Follow the arrow to the next box and copy your answer from the first box. Solve the next problem, follow the arrow, and copy your new answer in the next open box. Continue to solve the problems, copying each answer into the next box indicated by the arrow. When you've finished the puzzle correctly, your final answer should be the exact number needed to solve the final problem. Go on to the second puzzle and follow the same steps you used to work your way through the first one!

★
63.27
.359
4.226
43.3
+ 47.356

− 94.076

− 59.735

× 2.5

5) [ ]

× 4

9.4

Hint:
As you work through these problems, check your answers by using the reverse operation.
For example:
2.03 + 34.2 = 36.23
Check:
36.23 − 34.2 = 2.03

★
3.4
563.0
.345
22.22
+ 6.8

− 591.320

× 6

− 19.02

5) [ ]

× 6.6

− 9.999

0.099

Name____________________ Date ________

DECIMALS

2 x 3-digit multiplication

Coded Riddle

Why did the doughnut makers finally close their shop?

To figure out this riddle, solve the following problems and find your answers in the code boxes below. Write the letter from each problem in the code box with the matching answer. If the answer appears in more than one code box, fill in each box with the same letter.

F	**L**	**B**	**S**
0.38 × 29	87 × 0.9	584 × 0.6	4.38 × 29

H	**R**	**E**	**Y**
5.05 × 87	0.87 × 38	7.37 × 43	49.4 × 76

I	**P**	**D**	**W**
3.77 × 65	594 × 6.6	3.39 × 93	77.7 × 48

N	**U**	**O**	**T**
43.7 × 38	562 × 8.4	2.24 × 68	39.7 × 78

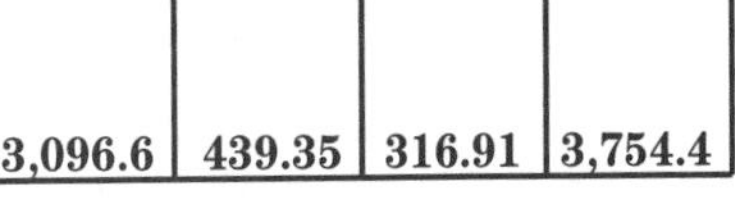

3,096.6	439.35	316.91	3,754.4

3,729.6	316.91	33.06	316.91

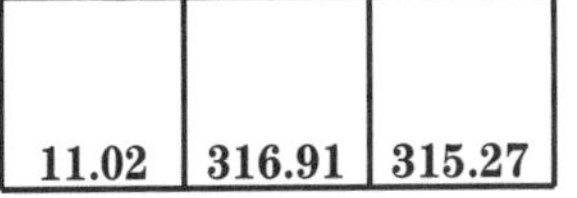

11.02	316.91	315.27

4,720.8	3,920.4

3,729.6	245.05	3,096.6	439.35

3,096.6	439.35	316.91

439.35	152.32	78.3	316.91

350.4	4,720.8	127.02	245.05	1,660.6	316.91	127.02	127.02

Name________________________________ Date __________

DECIMALS

Multiple step operations

Decimal Fun

Solve each problem by working from left to right. When you finish a problem, locate the answer in a box below, then write the letter above the answer. If the answer appears in more than one box, fill in each one with the same letter.

Take **47**	→ Subtract **6.55**	→ Add **0.22**	→ Multiply by **0.7**	= ________	= **R**
Take **8.63**	→ Add **26.4**	→ Multiply by **35**	→ Subtract **16.5**	= ________	= **T**
Take **13.779**	→ Multiply by **8**	→ Subtract **4.662**	→ Add **39.44**	= ________	= **N**
Take **58.2**	→ Add **66.489**	→ Subtract **123.457**	→ Add **8**	= ________	= **S**
Take **5.5**	→ Add **4.505**	→ Multiply by **7**	→ Subtract **20**	= ________	= **C**
Take **2.2**	→ Multiply by **8.4**	→ Subtract **1.477**	→ Add **0.33**	= ________	= **D**
Take **589**	→ Subtract **9.87**	→ Multiply by **0.4**	→ Add **0.048**	= ________	= **H**
Take **22.2**	→ Add **9.8**	→ Multiply by **6.5**	→ Subtract **0.65**	= ________	= **I**
Take **88.8**	→ Multiply by **0.4**	→ Subtract **15.32**	→ Add **50.8**	= ________	= **E**
Take **799**	→ Subtract **763.4**	→ Add **8.4**	→ Multiply by **9**	= ________	= **G**

Why did the hen always lift eggs?

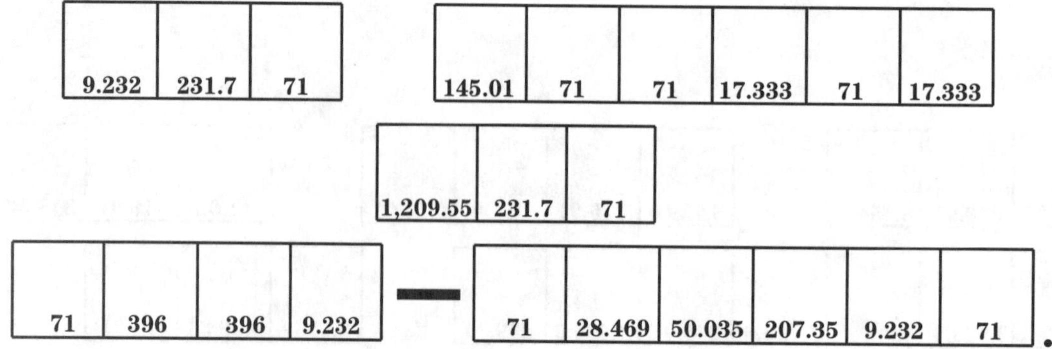

Name______________________________ Date __________

DECIMALS

Order of operations

Shapely Math #2

Study the shapes in equations 1–6. Each shape has only one match in the number grids. Use the shapes to fill in the missing numbers in the equations. Solve each number sentence. Check your answers against the scrambled answers in the Answer Box.

66	6.38	.007
4.3	84.1	.407
35.4	4.01	6.7

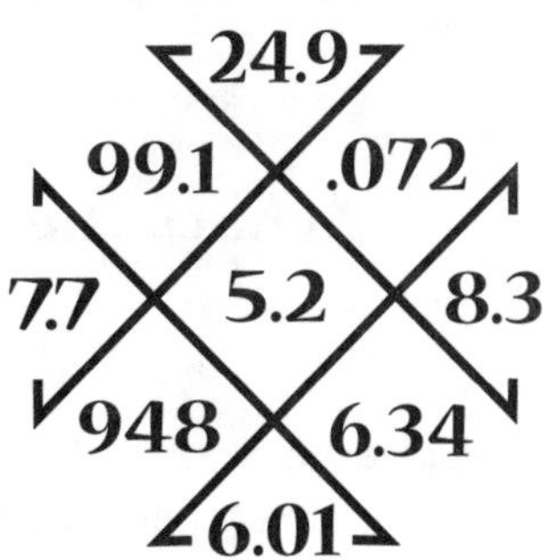

1. (___ − 4.01) + (35.4 − ___) = ______

2. (___ − ___) + (___ − ___) = ______

3. (___ − ___) + (___ − ___) = ______

4. (___ − ___) + (___ − ___) = ______

5. (___ − ___) + (___ − ___) = ______

6. (___ − ___) + (___ − ___) = ______

ANSWER BOX

593.6	69.3	953.926
16.0	30.49	11.34
1.665	18.66	33.47

Name________________________ Date __________

DECIMALS

No Kidding!

Order of operations

What's the tallest building in town?

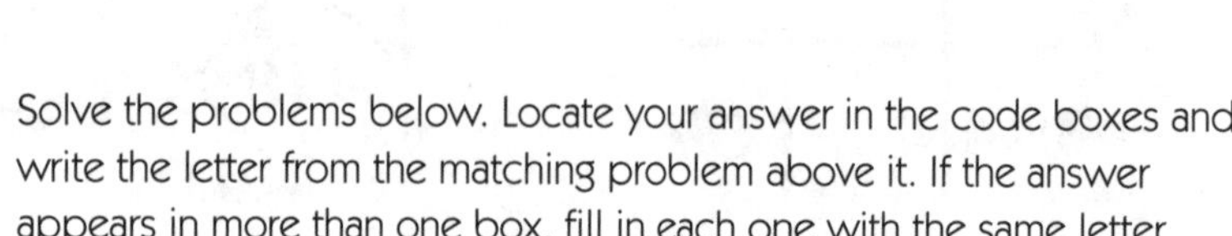

Solve the problems below. Locate your answer in the code boxes and write the letter from the matching problem above it. If the answer appears in more than one box, fill in each one with the same letter.

(0.5 x 3) + 0.3 = C	**C** = ________	(S x 0.9) + 0.2 = 4.7	**S** = ________
(6 x 0.3) + 2.5 = M	**M** = ________	(0.7 x 0.7) + 0.12 = E	**E** = ________
(8 x 0.6) + R = 5.0	**R** = ________	(2.2 x 4) + 0.7 = A	**A** = ________
(0.3 x 0.3) + 0.23 = H	**H** = ________	(8 x 0.7) + L = 6.3	**L** = ________
(7 x 7) + I = 49.3	**I** = ________	(0.4 x 0.8) + 0.07 = Y	**Y** = ________
(0.4 x B) + 0.03 = 0.19	**B** = ________	(0.9 x 0.5) + O = 0.49	**O** = ________
(9 x 0.3) + U = 3.5	**U** = ________	(T x 0.9) + 0.4 = 7.6	**T** = ________

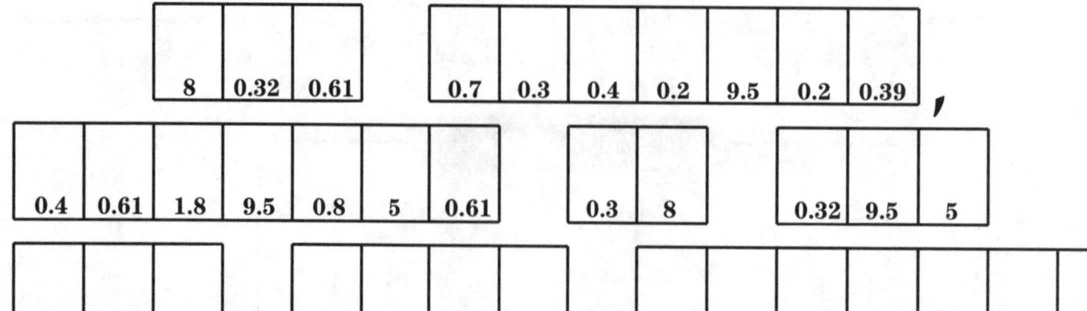

Name________________________ Date __________

Hidden Question and Answer #1

Locating ordered pairs

Read the ordered pairs (for example, 0,2) listed in the code boxes below. Find the letter of the alphabet that names each point given. Write the correct letter in the box above the ordered pair. Reveal a hidden question and answer.

R S N
H
O E
D M L
I
K G
Y (0,2) W
T
A (2,0) B

0 1 2 3 4 5 6 7 8 9 10 11

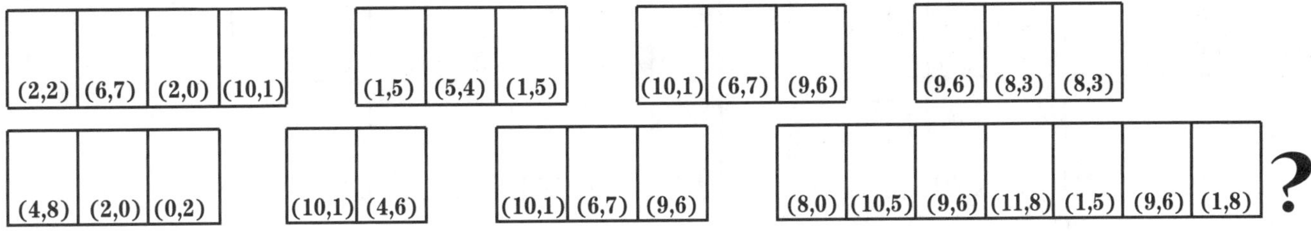

Answer

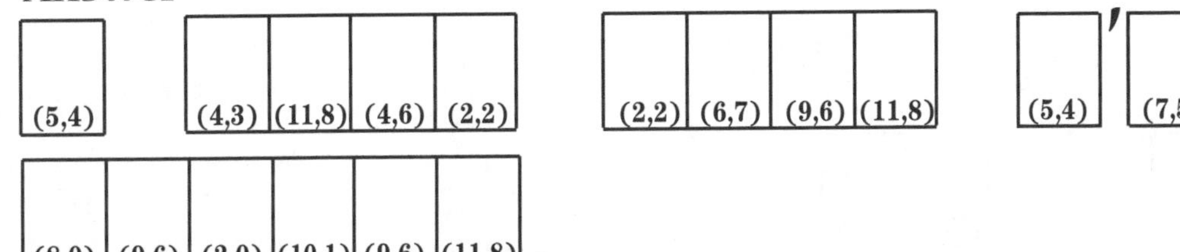

Name____ Date __________

Hidden Question and Answer #2

Locating ordered pairs

Read the ordered pairs (for example, 0,1) listed in the code boxes below. Find the letter of the alphabet that names each point given. Write the correct letter in the box above the ordered pair. Reveal a hidden question and answer.

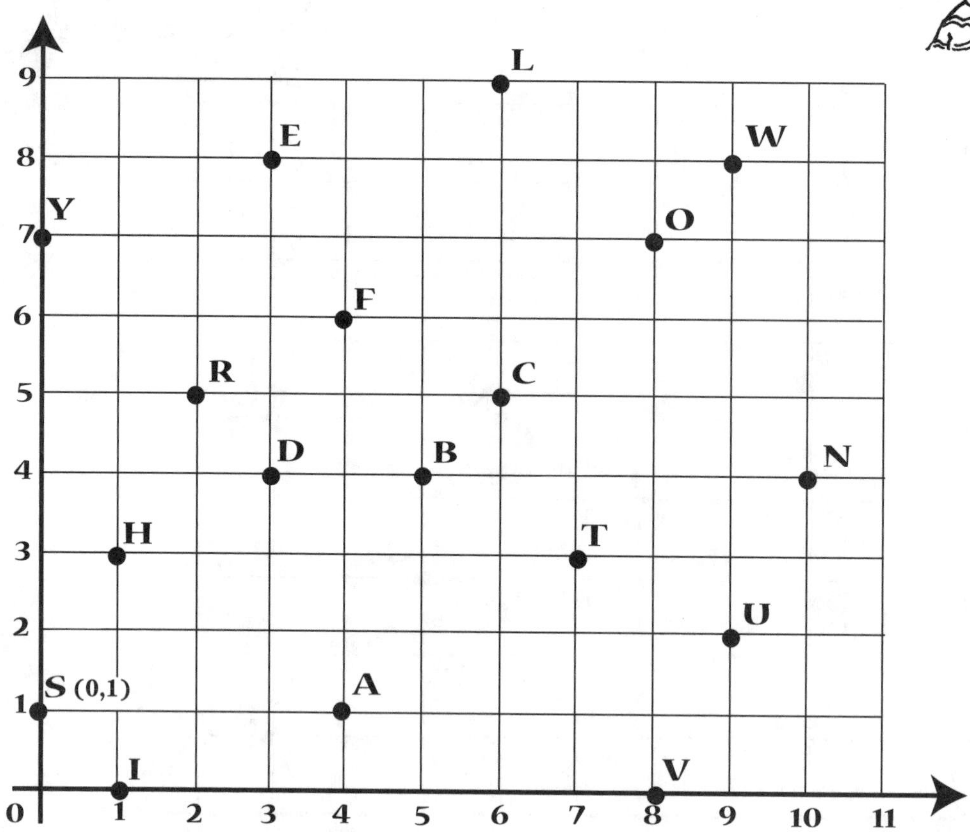

Question

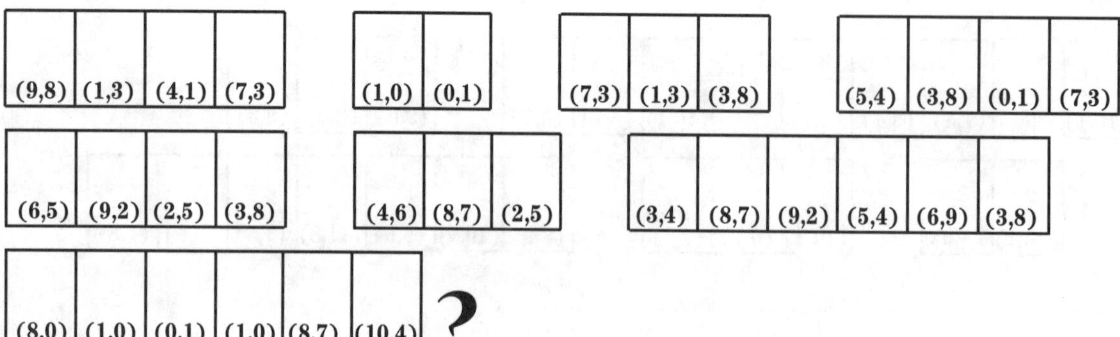

Answer

(0,1) (1,3) (9,2) (7,3)

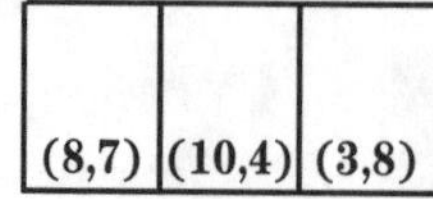

(3,8) (0,7) (3,8) .

Name_______________________________________ Date ________

TIME

Converting hours, minutes, and seconds

A Timely Puzzle

Write the answer to each problem in the space provided. Locate your answer in the boxes below, then write the word that is next to your answer in that box. Continue answering all the questions until you have decoded the following riddle:

Why did the downhill skier wear just one boot?

1. If you fall asleep at 9:15 P.M. and you wake up at 9:15 A.M., how many minutes did you sleep? = ____________ = **That**
2. If it's 6:15 A.M., what will the time be 46 minutes later? = ____________ = **The**
3. A diver holds his breath for 186 seconds. How many minutes and seconds is that? = ____________ = **The**
4. Mom's commute to work takes 46 minutes and she arrives at work at 8:20 A.M. When did she leave home? = ____________ = **One**
5. You leave the house at 8:12 A.M. and arrive at school at 8:31 A.M. How many seconds did it take you to get there? = ____________ = **Heard**
6. Sunrise is at 6:13 A.M. and sunset is at 7:16 P.M. How many hours and minutes of sunlight did we have? = ____________ = **Snow**
7. How many minutes have elapsed between 9:00 A.M. and 11:12 A.M.? = ____________ = **Foot**
8. If your gym, music, art, and math classes are 40 minutes each, what is the total number of hours and minutes? = ____________ = **Trail**
9. Two race car drivers finished a race in 46 minutes 30 seconds and 43 minutes 29 seconds, respectively. How much faster was the winner? = ____________ = **He**
10. If the fire drill interrupted class for 15 minutes, how many seconds of class did you miss? = ____________ = **Along**
11. If it's 3:30 P.M., how much time has passed since 1:25 P.M.? = ____________ = **Deep**
12. It takes 12 minutes and 36 seconds to walk around the city block. How many seconds did it take? = ____________ = **Was**

3 minutes, 1 second	1,140 seconds	720 minutes	7:01 A.M.
13 hours, 3 minutes	900 seconds	3 minutes, 6 seconds	2 hours, 40 minutes
756 seconds	7:34 A.M.	132 minutes	2 hours, 5 minutes

Answers

Reveal a Historical Fact (page 5)

1.	2,611	**6.**	48,907,816
2.	34,089	**7.**	508,798
3.	626,854	**8.**	80,116,211
4.	8,008	**9.**	7,707
5.	6,534,211	**10.**	29,648

The Greek and Roman god of sun and youth was Apollo.

Cross-Number Puzzle (page 6)

ACROSS	DOWN
1. 4,703	**1.** 493,666
3. 2,435	**2.** 50,930
4. 5,009	**4.** 56,934
5. 164,593	**6.** 6,451
6. 604,590	**8.** 9,443
7. 85,396	**9.** 25,793
11. 546,371	**10.** 81,247
12. 348,007	

+	39	23	17	42	68	94	75	56	83	49	32	95	57	71	63
5	44	28	22	47	73	99	80	61	88	54	37	100	62	76	68
8	47	31	25	50	76	102	83	64	91	57	40	103	65	79	71
4	43	27	21	46	72	98	79	60	87	53	36	99	61	75	67
7	46	30	24	49	75	101	82	63	90	56	39	102	64	78	70
9	48	32	26	51	77	103	84	65	92	58	41	104	66	80	72
2	41	25	19	44	70	96	77	58	85	51	34	97	59	73	65
6	45	29	23	48	74	100	81	62	89	55	38	101	63	77	69
1	40	24	18	43	69	95	76	57	84	50	33	96	58	72	64
3	42	26	20	45	71	97	78	59	86	52	35	98	60	74	66

58 Errors (page 7)

What always goes to bed with shoes on? *Horse*

Break the Code (page 8)

ACROSS	DOWN
2. 2,393	**1.** 2,281
4. 2,271	**2.** 2,126
5. 2,315	**3.** 3,351
6. 2,186	**6.** 2,625
8. 24,636	**7.** 2,620

What word has two vowels, two consonants, and two vowels—all in a row? *Bookkeeper*

"Sum" Number Search (page 9)

1. 17,384	**2.** 19,841	**3.** 19,755
4. 25,641	**5.** 20,964	**6.** 25,538
7. 14,192	**8.** 26,410	**9.** 19,108
10. 22,157	**11.** 20,409	**12.** 28,124

2	0	9	6	4	2	6	4	1	0
5	6	9	3	1	7	3	8	4	9
6	2	2	1	5	7	3	7	1	6
4	5	8	0	2	0	4	0	9	4
1	9	8	4	1	2	8	1	2	4
6	0	1	9	7	5	5	5	7	1
2	5	5	3	8	1	9	1	0	8

***What's the Difference?* Number Search** (page 10)

1. 3,369	**2.** 4,125	**3.** 4,974
4. 3,559	**5.** 2,134	**6.** 2,559
7. 991	**8.** 7,714	**9.** 6,605
10. 1,558	**11.** 2,446	**12.** 572
13. 570	**14.** 9010	**15.** 2,371

7	6	0	6	4	3	5	7	2	4	7
7	3	3	6	9	5	7	1	5	5	8
1	6	6	0	7	9	0	5	5	3	2
4	1	2	5	4	7	8	2	9	9	1
6	9	9	0	1	0	2	4	4	6	3
3	5	5	9	6	2	3	7	1	5	4

Last Number – First Number #1 (page 11)

1. 23,314	**2.** 43,363	**3.** 36,427
4. 72,905	**5.** 51,048	**6.** 87,332
7. 21,411	**8.** 15,204	**9.** 46,372
10. 27,326	**11.** 60,217	**12.** 75,268

What geometric figure never makes a mistake? *A right angle*

Solve the Mystery (page 12)

ACROSS	DOWN
1. 13,109	**2.** 31,922
5. 16,357	**3.** 27,309
6. 20,492	**4.** 44,418
7. 40,617	**5.** 12,222
9. 5,205	**8.** 3,552

What illness is difficult to discuss until it's completely cured? *Laryngitis*

What's the Difference Between Land and Sea? (page 13)

E 1,881	P 12,003	I 6,541
A 12,037	O 3,005	R 13,555
N 1,974	T 9,999	M 1,001
D 17,006	H 1,004	W 11,132
L 1,181	Y 11,311	S 652

The land is dirt-y and the sea is tide-y.

Cross Them Out #1 (page 14)

1. 13,525	**2.** 3,689	**3.** 12,521
4. 1,031	**5.** 12,221	**6.** 1,515
7. 16,290	**8.** 1,090	**9.** 10,151
10. 6,074	**11.** 7,573	**12.** 3,145

What's the difference between a sailo and a bargain hunter? *One sails the seas, the other sees the sales.*

59 Errors (page 15)

x	9	6	3	1	0	8	7	2	5	4	3	8	4	9	0	6	7	5
7	63	42	21	7	0	56	49	14	35	28	21	56	28	63	0	42	49	35
3	27	18	9	3	0	24	21	6	15	12	9	24	12	27	0	18	21	15
1	9	6	3	1	0	8	7	2	5	4	3	8	4	9	0	6	7	5
8	72	48	24	8	0	64	56	16	40	32	24	64	32	72	0	48	56	40
6	54	36	18	6	0	48	42	12	30	24	18	48	24	54	0	36	42	30
4	36	24	12	4	0	32	28	8	20	16	12	32	16	36	0	24	28	20
9	81	54	27	9	0	72	63	18	45	36	27	72	36	81	0	54	63	45
2	18	12	6	2	0	16	14	4	10	8	6	16	8	18	0	12	14	10
5	45	30	15	5	0	40	35	10	25	20	15	40	20	45	0	30	35	25

What is too much for one, enough fo two, and nothing at all for three? *Secret*

What a Mix-Up (page 16)

x	5	8	2	6
3	15	24	6	18
9	45	72	18	54
4	20	32	8	24
7	35	56	14	42

x	5	4	6	3
7	35	28	42	21
9	45	36	54	27
2	10	8	12	6
8	40	16	48	24

Note: There can be more than one solution to the following 2 boxes.

x	9	6	1	5
4	36	24	4	20
2	18	12	2	10
8	72	48	8	40
3	27	18	3	15

x	10	7	3	8
2	20	14	6	16
1	10	7	3	8
6	60	42	18	48
5	50	35	15	40

Solve the Riddle (page 17)

K 738	R 24,210	E 2,871	N 40,03
D 28,084	L 65,142	T 7,992	H 12,42
I 35,805	B 48,120	P 5,247	A 2,901
M 4,256	Y 54,351	W 4,130	O 9,732

Do you know what Mary had when she went out to dinner? *People know Mary had a little lamb.*

Cross Them Out #2 (page 18)

1. 38,556	**2.** 21,276	**3.** 16,842
4. 28,020	**5.** 39,906	**6.** 61,104
7. 9,999	**8.** 56,623	**9.** 39,192

What did the father say to his son who wanted to be a tank driver when he grew up? *I certainly won't stand in your way.*

atch It #1 (page 19)

1. 1,674 **2.** 2,436 **3.** 736
4. 4,508 **5.** 2,640 **6.** 2,520
7. 2,961 **8.** 806 **9.** 1,152
0. 2,166 **11.** 2,378 **12.** 3,528

Where does a frog change its clothes? *In a croak room*

ecret Code Time (page 20)

2,546	U 1,200	N 4,700	L 1,674
1,855	T 2,291	D 1,972	O 3,239
4,620	J 1,128	E 2,294	F 2,700
600	S 3,496	A 4,512	H 4,524

Why did Godzilla eat Tokyo instead of Rome? *He just was not in the mood for Italian food.*

onster Mystery (page 21)

ACROSS	DOWN
1. 24,576	**1.** 21,682
5. 56,296	**2.** 76,632
6. 61,386	**3.** 26,880
8. 30,272	**4.** 12,600
9. 44,154	**7.** 15,255

What did the hungry monster eat after the dentist pulled its tooth? *The dentist*

ast Number – First Number #2 (page 22)

1. 18,213 **2.** 33,856
3. 60,905 **4.** 51,646
5. 60,092 **6.** 23,161
7. 13,143 **8.** 32,076
9. 63,714 **10.** 42,413
1. 39,774 **12.** 43,831

What does the announcer say to start a flea race? *One, Two, Flea – GO!*

qual Values (page 23)

246	125	264	222	176
144	99	102	483	420
290	90	240	64	210
216	95	48	156	45

99	64	290	48	45
420	483	90	222	125
246	156	95	144	216
102	240	176	264	210

What's the best way to double your money? *If you fold the five-dollar bill, you double it. But if you open it up again, you'll find it increases.*

***Did You Hear?* Riddles** (page 24)

W 38	O 69	D 222	L 686
T 54	M 521	Y 681	H 468
S 442	A 588	F 123	U 55
N 655	I 515	L 232	I 122

About your muscles? Never Mind – *it's a lot of mush.*

About the rotten pudding? Never Mind – *you wouldn't swallow it.*

Remainders (page 25)

ACROSS	DOWN
1. 78r6	**1.** 92r7
2. 48r5	**2.** 49r4
3. 69r3	**3.** 90r2
5. 89r1	**4.** 67r8
6. 38r2	**7.** 65r2
7. 96r3	**8.** 88r7

Match It #2 (page 26)

1. 583 **2.** 246 **3.** 339 **4.** 949
5. 443 **6.** 409 **7.** 560 **8.** 300
9. 764 **10.** 226 **11.** 793 **12.** 415

What do you give a seasick elephant? *Plenty of room*

99s (page 27)

1. 23r30 **2.** 56r48 **3.** 71r31
4. 64r42 **5.** 37r17 **6.** 88r52
7. 49r39 **8.** 57r23 **9.** 76r24

More *Did You Hear?* Riddles (page 28)

P 13	A 75	T 68	H 86
R 22	O 41	U 20	K 80
Y 40	I 83	M 43	C 35
S 38	C 39	E 21	N 66

About the rotten food? Never mind – *it turns my stomach.*

About the chef who dropped the egg? Never mind – *it cracks me up.*

Follow the Arrows #1 (page 29)

A 18,931 ➤4,458 ➤2,229 ➤11,145 ➤4,210 ➤842

B 24,244 ➤451 ➤17,589 ➤5,214 ➤869 ➤46,926 ➤5,551

Links (page 30)

N 80 D 1,098 L 44 G 847 Y 231
A 77 S 36 B 1,060 U 183 O 105

What strange children live in the ocean? *Buoys and gulls*

Shapely Math #1 (page 31)

1. (48 × 44) ÷ (68 – 63) = **422 r2**
2. (22 × 75) ÷ (68 – 22) = **35 r40**
3. (63 × 84) ÷ (39 – 35) = **1,323**
4. (48 × 24) ÷ (97 – 91) = **192**
5. (32 × 74) ÷ (63 – 57) = **394 r4**
6. (39 × 91) ÷ (91 – 84) = **507**

Elephant Trivia (page 32)

J 84	I 113	K 81	A 112
L 85	T 91	E 90	R 149
O 104	S 165	N 64	
D 72	W 159	H 50	

Why did the elephant cross the road? *He didn't want to hear that last joke.*

Riddle Time (page 33)

T 48	K 7
G 34	C 31
E 36	H 9
A 6	N 40
F 68	S 8
W 5	P 25
I 33	O 26

What has 500 teeth and says "Beware of Dog"? *A picket fence with a sign on it*

Equal Values (page 34)

$\frac{5}{3}=1\frac{2}{3}$	$\frac{14}{10}=1\frac{4}{10}=1\frac{2}{5}$	$\frac{9}{6}=1\frac{3}{6}=1\frac{1}{2}$	$\frac{8}{5}=1\frac{3}{5}$
$\frac{13}{8}=1\frac{5}{8}$	$\frac{17}{14}=1\frac{3}{14}$	$\frac{7}{4}=1\frac{3}{4}$	$\frac{17}{12}=1\frac{5}{12}$
$\frac{12}{7}=1\frac{5}{7}$	$\frac{10}{8}=1\frac{2}{8}=1\frac{1}{4}$	$\frac{9}{4}=2\frac{1}{4}$	$\frac{11}{6}=1\frac{5}{6}$
$\frac{9}{7}=1\frac{2}{7}$	$\frac{5}{2}=2\frac{1}{2}$	$\frac{12}{9}=1\frac{3}{9}=1\frac{1}{3}$	$\frac{13}{12}=1\frac{1}{12}$

What is the difference between a football player and a duck? *A football player is found in a huddle, but a duck is found in a puddle.*

A Sharp Riddle (page 35)

D $1\frac{1}{6}$	E $\frac{1}{3}$	F $\frac{7}{20}$	S $\frac{1}{2}$
T $\frac{3}{10}$	O $2\frac{1}{6}$	R $1\frac{7}{24}$	Y $\frac{7}{30}$
I $\frac{5}{6}$	H $\frac{1}{4}$	L $1\frac{1}{3}$	C $\frac{11}{24}$
U $\frac{2}{15}$	K $1\frac{5}{12}$	W $\frac{4}{21}$	N $\frac{13}{14}$

If two vampires had a race, who would win? *Neither—they would finish neck-in-neck.*

Wrestle the Code (page 36)

E	$\frac{1}{2}$	A	$\frac{3}{4}$
D	$\frac{1}{3}$	R	$2\frac{1}{3}$
T	$\frac{2}{3}$	O	$\frac{1}{6}$
S	$1\frac{1}{5}$	W	$2\frac{1}{4}$
Y	1	N	$1\frac{1}{3}$
I	$1\frac{1}{2}$	L	3
H	$1\frac{2}{3}$	F	$\frac{6}{7}$
		G	$\frac{5}{9}$

What did the wrestler say when he sat down to eat at the buffet? *I really don't want all this food to go to waist.*

Decimal Match (page 37)

1. 0.3 **2.** 13.001 **3.** 4.04 **4.** 7.015
5. 13.01 **6.** 4.004 **7.** 0.03 **8.** 13.1
9. 4.040 **10.** 13.10 **11.** 4.4 **12.** 7.15

How do we know football referees are happy? *We know referees are happy because they always whistle while they work.*

Follow the Arrows #2 (page 38)

A 158.511 ➤64.435 ➤4.7 ➤11.75 ➤2.35 ➤9.4

B 595.765 ➤4.445 ➤26.67 ➤7.65 ➤1.53 ➤10.098 ➤0.099

Coded Riddle (page 39)

F 11.02	L 78.3	B 350.4
S 127.02	H 439.35	R 33.06
E 316.91	Y 3,754.4	I 245.05
P 3,920.4	D 315.27	W 3,729.6
N 1,660.6	U 4,720.8	O 152.32
T 3,096.6		

Why did the doughnut makers finally close their shop? *They were fed up with the hole business.*

Decimal Fun (page 40)

R 28.469	T 1,209.55	N 145.01
S 9.232	C 50.035	D 17.333
H 231.7	I 207.35	E 71
G 396		

Why did the hen always lift eggs? *She needed the eggs-ercise.*

1. (4.3 - [4.01]) + ([35.4] - 5.2) = **30.49**

2. (.072 - .007) + (8.3 - 6.7) = **1.665**

3. (99.1 - 66) + (6.38 - 6.01) = **33.47**

4. (99.1 - 84.1) + (7.7 - 6.7) = **16**

5. (948 - .007) + (6.34 - .407) = **953.926**

6. (24.9 - 4.3) + (84.1 - 35.4) = **69.3**

No Kidding! (page 42)

C 1.8	S 5	M 4.3	E 0.61
R 0.2	A 9.5	H 0.32	L 0.7
I 0.3	Y 0.39	B 0.4	O 0.04
U 0.8	T 8		

What's the tallest building in town? *The library, because it has the most stories.*

Hidden Question and Answer #1 (page 43)

Y (0,2)	A (2,0)	I (5,4)
B (8,0)	N (11,8)	R (1,8)
S (4,8)	H (6,7)	E (9,6)
D (1,5)	O (4,6)	M (7,5)
L (10,5)	W (2,2)	K (4,3)
G (8,3)	T (10,1)	

Question: *What did the egg say to the blender?*

Answer: *I know when I'm beaten.*

Hidden Question and Answer #2 (page 44)

Y (0,7)	R (2,5)	A (4,1)
T (7,3)	U (9,2)	S (0,1)
E (3,8)	B (5,4)	O (8,7)
N (10,4)	H (1,3)	D (3,4)
L (6,9)	V (8,0)	I (1,0)
F (4,6)	C (6,5)	W (9,8)

Question: *What is the best cure for double vision?*
Answer: *Shut one eye.*

A Timely Puzzle (page 45)

1. 720 minutes **2.** 7:01 A.M.
3. 3 minutes, 6 seconds **4.** 7:34 A.M.
5. 1,140 seconds **6.** 13 hours, 3 minutes
7. 132 minutes **8.** 2 hours, 40 minutes
9. 3 minutes, 1 second **10.** 900 seconds
11. 2 hours, 5 minutes **12.** 756 seconds

Why did the downhill skier wear just one boot? *He heard that the snow along the trail was one foot deep.*